D0210292

GOOD-BYE

to

SHY

---

85 Shybusters That Work!

LEIL LOWNDES

McGraw-Hill

New York   Chicago   San Francisco   Lisbon   London   Madrid   Mexico City
Milan   New Delhi   San Juan   Seoul   Singapore   Sydney   Toronto

*The **McGraw·Hill** Companies*

Library of Congress Cataloging-in-Publication Data

Lowndes, Leil.
    Good-bye to shy : 85 shybusters that work! / by Leil Lowndes.
        p.   cm.
    Includes index.
    ISBN 0-07-145642-2 (alk. paper)
    1. Bashfulness.   I. Title.

  BF575.B3L69   2006
  155.2'32—dc22   2006012763

2 3 4 5 6 7 8 9 0   CUS/CUS   0 9 8 7 6

ISBN 0-07-145642-2

McGraw-Hill books are available at special quantity discounts to use as premiums and sales promotions, or for use in corporate training programs. For more information, please write to the Director of Special Sales, Professional Publishing, McGraw-Hill, Two Penn Plaza, New York, NY 10121-2298. Or contact your local bookstore.

This book is printed on acid-free paper.

Good-Bye to Shy is dedicated to those who know the
anguish of shyness that I, too, suffered for many years.

Contents

⑥ For Big-Time Sufferers: Get a (New) Life 107

⑦ Parties and Other Places in Hell   115

⑧ Fearless Conversation   133

9 ● Eight Advanced, Sure-Fire Shy Extinguishers   163

10 ● Sex and the Single Shy   185

Preface

Shyness is a curse. Shyness makes me feel like I am an unwanted guest in everyone else's world. Shyness is the worst personality trait of all, without a doubt. I would rather be obnoxious and boorish than shy. Obnoxious and boorish people don't seem to be too bothered by being obnoxious and boorish at least.

—Dave B., Toledo, Ohio

Think back to your grandparents' time, when online dating was a twinkle in some yet-unborn techie's eyes and the words *pick up* meant "get your socks up off the floor." If Grandma had been too shy to go to parties and Grandpa hid out in the bedroom memorizing guests' coat labels, you wouldn't be here reading this book.

Things haven't changed all that much for Shys over the years. Well-meaning friends and family still say, "C'mon, just force yourself to . . . go to the party . . . ask her for a date . . . talk to him . . . request a raise . . . join the conversation . . . speak up in the meeting. . . ."

Don't they know how hard it is? The anxiety? The wanting to be invisible? The fear that you'll say something stupid? The sparkling conversations in your head that you don't have the courage to start? Yet you know you have a lot to offer and, if you could just say "good-bye" to being shy, everything would be OK. You could get on with your life.

I know firsthand how excruciating shyness is. Well into my working years, my face looked like a radish whenever I talked to strangers. I remember standing on the sidelines at parties wishing my dress matched the wallpaper to make me invisible.

I wish I'd had this book then. I am gratified that I can provide it for you now.

NEW FINDINGS ON SHYNESS

Research in the 1940s gave us a gift that saved millions of lives–penicillin. Research in recent years has given us a gift that can save millions the agony of shyness. It derives from recent studies on shyness conducted by pioneering researchers in sociology, psychiatry, genetics, biology, physiology, and pharmacology.

Shyness research is almost synonymous with the names Philip Zimbardo, Bernardo Carducci, Jerome Kagan, and a few others. I am grateful to them, and you will gain further insight from much of their groundbreaking research. All of the information in *Good-Bye to Shy* is substantiated by the recent work of professionals in both the medical and mental health fields. Based on their research, I've created eighty-five ShyBusters–exercises to cure or curtail your shyness. (If you'd like more information on any particular technique, you can go to the original sources, which are listed in the References.)

If you take time to practice each ShyBuster, your shyness will soon be a faint memory. I know, because I went from a hermit-teen who was terrified of people to a self-assured woman who now lectures around the country, does media interviews, and feels comfortable at any gathering. If these ShyBusters worked for a girl who was shy around her own shadow, they will definitely work for you!

A few notes before you start. Recently, there have been phenomenal pharmacological advances to help people suffering from a vast variety of conditions. When I was battling shyness, "help in a capsule" didn't exist. I was a do-it-yourselfer and, in *Good-Bye to Shy*, I'm addressing other Shys who choose to take that path. If you are seeing a mental health professional, follow his or her advice on medication. It is not within the purview of this book to make suggestions either way.

Fellow do-it-yourselfers, here's how to get the most out of *Good-Bye to Shy*. First, read the whole book sequentially so that you understand the significance of each ShyBuster. Then, depending on which exercises are most challenging for you personally, decide the order you're going to do them in–easiest to most difficult, of course. And then get to work!

Don't skip Part 11, "For Parents and Shys Who Want to Know Why (and How to Prevent It!)." There you will find fascinating answers to questions about your own personal shyness. If you have children who are, or whom you fear will become shy, you will discover unique ways to prevent or shrink their shyness.

WHO YA GONNA BLAME?

When I was a kid, I had all of the usual questions: "Why is the sky blue?" "Did Eve have a belly button?" "What was the best thing before sliced bread?"

But "Why am I shy?" wasn't one of them. I didn't care why. I just wanted a quick cure. As a recovered Shy, however, I realize origins are important. They give you a realistic picture of yourself, of what to expect, and of how to go about it.

I've heard Shys speculate . . .

"It must have been Mom and Dad's fault."

"It was those nasty kids in the neighborhood who called me names."

"I think it's genetic."

Later in the book, I will give you clues to the origin of your particular shyness. But before I do so, I would like to quote a great actress and, I now discover, a great philosopher, who fought a lifelong battle with shyness.

We are taught you must blame your father, your sisters, your brothers, the school, the teachers. You can blame anyone, but never blame yourself. It's never your fault. But it's always your fault, because if you want to change, you're the one who has got to change. It's as simple as that, isn't it?

–Katharine Hepburn

As you will learn, the origins of shyness are different for each Shy. You will also discover what "type" of Shy you are. Are you, for example, a Highly Sensitive Shy (HSS), who was born with a proclivity toward timidity? Or are you a Situational Shy (SS), whose parents and youthful experiences deeply affected you?

I put this key section at the end of the book because, if you are like me when I was shy, you probably want to race right to the cures and will worry about "why" later on. If you want a deeper understanding of the techniques, however, you might want to read that section first.

SHYS SPEAK OUT

The stories throughout the book come from my own stinging shyness and the experiences of other Shys I've known. Other stories come from attendees in my shyness seminars. At first, I thought that inviting people to a "Shyness Seminar" would be like telling participants for a "Fear of Tigers" club to meet me in the tiger's cage at the zoo. Happily, however, Shys did come, and they shared their experiences openly.

I asked them to e-mail me their triumphs and tribulations so you can read them in their own words. You will also find excerpts from letters sent by readers of my other books and complimentary monthly e-zine (which you can sign up for by visiting my website, lowndes.com). At the end of the book, there is a list of names of those who contributed. Some contributors requested anonymity and they have chosen a substitute name.

Finally, let me introduce a few terms that I will use for the sake of simplicity. We'll substitute the word *Shys* for shy people, *Sures* for those who are confident, and *scary* for people or situations you find intimidating. And, for extra ease in reading, instead of constantly writing *he, she, they, some Shys, many Shys, most Shys,* and so on, may I substitute the word *you*? Not everything in *Good-Bye to Shy* will refer to you specifically, of course. So please don't take it personally if the word *you* sounds like I'm pointing fingers. The findings are based on studies and statistics of Shys in general. Here's the deal. I'll make the book easier for you to read, if you don't take offense when I say *you* meaning "in general," OK?

Now let's get started so that you, too, can soon say "good-bye" to your shyness.

I used to be very shy. I couldn't look people in the face and became red. I was embarrassed and used to sweat in front of others. Due to low self-esteem and low self-image, I used to feel inferior to others. But then one day, I began to question things. I realized that nobody is better than me. Who told me I'm no good? I realized that the people who make me feel that way are not in that credible or successful position themselves. So why would I believe what these people say about me? They were not qualified to make such comments.

—Tony V., Sydney, Australia

How to Deal with People *Now* Until Your Shyness Is Gone

OK, you say, "I know my shyness isn't going to vaporize like a falling star. Do I need to go on suffering until I've done all of the ShyBusters in the book?"

Like any goal worth attaining, of course, it will take time to gain complete confidence. But here's some good news: You will soon have four ways to deal with people *now* (and three ways to deal with yourself!) that will take the sting out of your shyness.

— • —

(1)

Should I Tell People I'm Shy?

"YOU, SHY? YOU'VE GOT TO BE KIDDING!"

It happens to all of us. Some well-meaning friend or family member blithely suggests, "Well, why don't you just tell people you're shy? Then you'll feel more comfortable around them."

So you consider it. You run a couple of scenarios through your mind:

If I tell them, will they say, "Oh, you poor dear, you're shy? I understand what an awful feeling that must be. Well, I certainly want to become your friend and help you get over it."

Don't think so.

If I share my secret with a potential romantic partner, will he or she say, "Oh, that's wonderful. I find shy people sooo sexy. Let's go out on a date and you can tell me all about it."

Not likely.

So, for the moment, you decide not to tell.

Wise choice! If you did, I know from experience exactly what you would hear. People would just laugh it off and say something like, "Oh, not you! You've got to be kidding. You're not shy. I mean you're so nice, so friendly." Yada yada yada. It happens all the time.

Let me interject an important note here. If, by chance, you are working with a therapist who encourages you to reveal your shyness, follow that counsel. Whatever your counselor advises overrides any suggestion in *Good-Bye to Shy*. Each Shy is different, and treatments vary.

I am teaching my way through graduate school. And on the surface, I guess I don't seem shy, but my timidness is so painful that in order to not have to speak to someone I will avoid them. In a group, I will just sit and listen (never putting in my opinion) to a conversation. Sometimes I tell people I'm shy, and they just laugh it off. They don't believe me. They don't know how much I'm suffering inside.

–Angela P., Hope, Arkansas

THE DAY I TOLD "MY SECRET"

In high school, my mother was anxious about my sagging self-esteem and lack of friends. One Sunday evening after dinner, Mama recommended that I tell the other girls that I was shy.

What, tell them? That was like telling a boxer to lean right into the punch. (The funny thing is that it works in boxing.) But telling people I was shy would have me down for the count.

"Promise me you will, Leilie?"

"Mama, I can't." She looked disappointed.

"I promise, Mama."

That night I lay awake, staring at the ceiling, mopping tears out of my ears, and planning how and when to divulge my "disgraceful secret."

The time came much too soon. While walking to gym class the next day, I said to myself, *now or never*. As I entered the locker room on D-Day (Divulge Day), Miss Popularity herself was already there. While donning our shorts and tees, Penelope started playing her favorite sport, small talk. That was my weakest game.

The Big Confession

"Well, Leilie, did you enjoy the weekend?"

My mind went into immediate self-conscious overdrive. *Should I tell her the truth, that I just hung around the house all by myself? Or should*

I fake an upbeat, "Oh, I had a fabulous time"? No, that's not a good strategy, because she might counter by asking me what I did.

By now, the unspoken time limit for a response, any response, was up. I returned her serve with an unskilled, "Uh, yeah."

Sure enough, she gave me the grand slam, "What did you do?" Now I faced sure defeat. It was a choice of fibbing or 'fessing up. Remembering my promise to Mama, I chose the latter.

I looked down at my sneakers and blurted out, "I'm shy." Penelope seemed surprised and volleyed back the expected: "What? Not you. You're not shy. You're kidding! I mean, you have no trouble talking to me. . . . Uh, well, see you later," she said, scurrying off to class.

I wondered if I'd done the right thing.

I got my answer twenty-four hours later, almost to the minute. When I arrived at gym class the next day, the girls were opening their lockers and chatting like magpies. "Hi, Leilie," one shouted across the locker room. "I hear you're shy. Is that true?"

Her comment was a cannonball in my stomach. As I was reeling from that one, another girl blasted me, "What have you got to be shy about?"

Babbling about being nauseous, I dashed out of the locker room, up the stairs, and into an empty classroom where I could hide my tears. I missed lunch that day but didn't care. I couldn't have eaten anyway.

In retrospect, I realize the locker-room gang didn't intend to be cruel. In fact, they were probably trying to make me feel at ease. But, like most people, they were unskilled at dealing with shyness. And, as hard as it is to believe, people who don't know you well don't care about your shyness anyway!

ShyBuster #1
Don't Tell Strangers

As a general rule, unless you've been advised otherwise by a responsible mental health professional, don't tell people that you're shy. Save the revelation for people who are important to you, like relatives or close friends.

②

How Savvy Shys Get Out of a Situation They Can't Face . . . Yet!

TELL THE HALF-TRUTH, THE HALF-TRUTH, AND NOTHING BUT THE HALF-TRUTH

As in anything, there are a few exceptions—and the "don't tell" rule is no exception. Situations may come up when you feel you must mention your shyness for a specific reason.

For example, suppose that a friend decides to invite a dozen people to her house to watch the Oscars. One person is buying the cheese and crackers. Another is bringing a few extra chairs. A few others are bringing pop and wine. She asks you to call some of the guests and invite them.

But you're too shy to talk to people you hardly know. Now you have a dilemma. Is it better to "confess" that you're shy? Or should you find another excuse for wriggling out of the request?

Neither, actually. Take the middle road and half tell your friend by *alluding* to your shyness in a lighthearted fashion. That way, you don't make her uncomfortable, yet she gets the point. You don't sound like you are declining the request just because you don't want the hassle.

In situations like this, go ahead and use the "S" word matter-of-factly. Just toss it off. Say something like, "Well, a shy girl like me couldn't talk to that many new people in one day." Or, "If you were as shy as I am, you'd rather die than make those calls." Then suggest some other way you can help.

"I'M SHY, SO WHAT'S THE BIG DEAL?"

You also might find yourself in a situation where you deem it best to mention your shyness up front. Perhaps you've been assigned to work on a project with a few colleagues or team members, and circumstances could come up where it might be best for them to know. In these cases, find a way to bring the subject up so it doesn't make any of you uncomfortable. During a casual conversation, for example, you might ask them if they've ever been shy. Then tell them that you are. But do it with a big smile and a "So what's the big deal?" attitude.

Divulge it with lightheartedness, like you're saying, "I feel fantastic today." People pay attention to your tone of voice and body language much more than your words. But you knew that already.

ShyBuster #3
Mention It with a "So What?" Attitude

Find an appropriate time in a conversation and introduce the subject of shy people. Toss your own shyness off casually, and it will slide off your listeners like a satin sheet. Having told them in a carefree manner could come in very handy later. When they ask you to do something or go somewhere, laughingly remind them, "C'mon, I told you I was shy." It sounds much better than, "I can't do that. I'm too shy."

Don't use this ShyBuster as a cop-out! It is only a temporary bandage until you can wear your "I'm Confident" button.

③

How to Battle the Blushing, Sweating, and Other Shy Signs

Some Shys sweat, blush, or exude other overt signs of shyness, so they figure they have to tell people they are shy. "Not ne-ces-sar-i-ly," as Freud said. Sometimes sweat is just sweat. Sometimes a blush is just a blush.

If you like, you can warn them about your "blushing problem" or whatever your particular symptom is. But there is no need to connect it with shyness. Shyness! What's that?

HIT IT RIGHT ON THE HEAD WITH HUMOR

It's not just Shys who suffer the soggy-mitt syndrome. Some very confident people blush, sweat, or have clammy hands, too. One of my clients is an extremely confident CEO, yet a profligate blusher.

Local television stations often invite Bernard to comment on the state of the economy. Being on TV is an intensely blush-generating situation. Bernard knows he'll have a crimson face during his interview. But he is not the least flustered by his blushing. He even seems to enjoy people razzing him.

Every time he arrives at the station for an interview, the man at the welcome desk pushes the intercom to announce: "Calling all makeup artists. Calling all makeup artists. Girls, get the extra pancake [cover-up makeup]. Bernie Blusher is here."

Bernard joins their laughter as people greet him in the hall, "Hi there, Red!" "How's it going, Rosy?" They're not bothered by it because they know he's not, either. Unself-consciously, Bernard had previously warned people that he might blush at any minute. He chuckles, "My wife hates having hot flashes, so I'm having them for her."

Bernard proudly calls himself the world's expert on blushing. Here are a few esoteric facts that may be of interest to other blushers: Blushing runs in families, but babies don't blush. Fifty-one percent of people blush, and many of them are not shy.[1] Women blush more than men, and people of all skin colors blush.

Bernard pretends to be jealous of his CFO, Jolan, a Native American. "He blushes worse than I do," he grumbles. "But nobody can see it!"

Are sweaty palms your problem? Before shaking hands, you can joke, "Wait a minute, let me dry my mitts off first or you're not going to like what you feel." Or you can say, "Shake at your own risk. My hands are always sopping." Highlight the *always*, and no one will connect it with shyness.

Home remedy hint: When I feared my hands would sweat profusely, I'd put antiperspirant and a dusting of powder on my hands. A little dab will do ya. (Just don't tell people what's on them.)

ShyBuster #4
Laugh About the Symptoms, Not the Shyness

If you know that some physical symptoms of your shyness will show, jokingly "warn" people of your incipient blush, mushy mitts, or sweaty flashes. No need to even mention that shyness is connected with it.

---

(4)

How to Talk to Yourself About Your Shyness

LABELS ARE LETHAL

You wouldn't scrawl "I am shy" on a heavy sandwich board and wear it around town. Revealing your shyness to too many people can drag you down just as much. Besides, labeling yourself *shy* is inaccurate. You are a complex mixture of an immeasurable number of qualities. To choose just one puts unnecessary emphasis on it.

Calling yourself shy could also be a perilously self-fulfilling prophesy. When you tell people you're shy, you are not just telling others. You are telling yourself as well. *And you are the person who really counts.*

When a Label Stopped the Music for Me

I don't think I was destined to be a singing diva. However, someone slapped a label across my lips when I was in the seventh grade. Nary an on-key note has come out of my mouth since then.

In seventh grade, I sang in the church choir. One afternoon during a rocky rehearsal, the choirmaster turned his stern face directly toward me: "*Someone* is off-key. I want that *someone* to just mouth the words." There was no mistaking who that off-key someone was. From that day on, I sang like a crow with a cold. To this day, with great embarrassment, I silently mouth the words to "Happy Birthday."

A few years ago, I was listening to the radio with an old classmate who knew I was severely musically challenged. The station was playing the Top 40 songs that were popular when I was in sixth grade. Just for fun, I started warbling along with the radio. When I'd finished, my friend said,

"Leil, that's perfect!"

"Perfect what?"

"Perfect pitch."

"Couldn't be."

" 'Twas!"

Tentatively, I tried a few more songs from my pre–seventh grade years. We were both staggered because I was right on-key. But here's the mind-boggler. I could not sing even one song that came after that fateful "someone is off-key" day.

The choir master had *labeled* me tone-deaf. Therefore, I was tone-deaf–a self-fulfilling prophesy.

I'M JUST CARRYING ONE MORE PIECE OF BAGGAGE

The American Association of People with Disabilities doesn't let their members burn themselves with the "handicapped" branding iron. They wisely decree, "Someone in a wheelchair is not 'handicapped' or 'disabled.' They are just like able-bodied people. They simply carry one more piece of baggage, their disability."[2] Some members ask people not to use the word *handicapped* in their presence.

Don't call yourself shy. Think of yourself as a self-assured person who carries a surplus bag–one you'll soon shed–called "Shyness."

We all have little voices inside of us. They can be nasty, but powerful. They can destroy your self-worth by calling you names. Slaughter them immediately! Never say "I am shy" to yourself. Instead, say "The ShyBusters are working, and I'm soon going to be confident."

DON'T USE THE "S" WORD AROUND ME!

It's not only when you're a kid that hearing people refer to you as shy is destructive. It's a punch in your ego at any age. Think about it. You could be the most fabulous-looking person to grace the planet, but if enough people called you ugly, you'd start to believe it.

It's not only your inner voices that you must silence. Outlaw using the "S" word with the outer voices that you hear every day–that means your mother, father, sisters, brothers, kids, nephews, nieces, cousins, and friends. Don't let them call you shy to your face–or behind your back.

ShyBuster #6
Forbid Family and Friends to Call You "Shy"

Every time someone says, "Don't be shy," or asks, "Why are you so shy?" they're digging the hole deeper for you. Sometimes they think they're helping when they add, "You don't have anything to be shy about."

No way. They are not doing you any favors. It's even worse when you overhear them telling someone else that you're shy. Ban the "S" word in your household as strongly as you would @#%!.

When the Going Gets Tough

FIND A WAY TO "WORK AROUND" IT

Even though I was no longer shy by the time I made the breakthrough discovery of how any molecules of musical ability were smashed by the choirmaster, I still felt insecure about being in a group where people were singing.

Resolving to take the agony out of just mouthing songs, I sat down, pen and paper in hand, and made a list of some of my positive qualities that could help me "work around" my coughing crow voice.

Actors in musical theater use the term *sell a song* when referring to performers who don't necessarily sing well but who make a song appealing by looking confident and using electrifying gestures.

Hey, I thought. *As a recovered Shy, I can do that. I can make eye contact with people and smile. I don't mind being looked at. I now have the courage to be playful, and (a real sign that I was cured) I even enjoy showing off occasionally.* In other words, I can "sell the song." I call this "working around" my musical insecurity.

The moment soon came to test the technique. I was at a birthday dinner for a good friend. The restaurant lights lowered. The pastry chef himself came in with a tall hat and a taller cake. We all jumped to our feet and began singing "Happy Birthday."

Wow, did I ham it up! I opened my mouth wide, smiled at everyone while "singing," and jokingly made conductor-like gestures. No one would ever dream that the sound coming out of my big mouth was . . . silence.

SHOW YOUR "GOOD STUFF"

Suppose that you must attend a gathering, but a wave of shyness engulfs you. To reduce your anxiety about the party, grab a pen and make a list of your positive qualities. Your list might go something like this:

1. I have excellent taste in clothes.
2. I love movies and have seen practically all of the current ones.
3. I'm really good at horseback riding.
4. I've been told that I have beautiful teeth.

When you've finished the list, imagine positive ways you can employ each quality at the event. For example,

1. **My taste in clothes:** I'll wear my new suit and look terrific.
2. **My knowledge about movies:** I'll bring up the subject by asking people if they recommend any current movies.
3. **My riding skill:** I'll ask people what activities or sports *they* enjoy. Then I can talk about horseback riding.
4. **My beautiful teeth:** I'll smile a lot!

Dreaming up ways to show off your positive qualities is a powerful weapon for fighting fear.

ShyBuster #7
Make a "Work-Around" List

Politicians and salespeople plan ways to bring the subject around to their interests. The next time you find yourself apprehensive about an upcoming situation, make a list of your positive qualities. When you've finished your list, actually plan how you can use each to your benefit.

What People *Really* Think of You

If you're like most Shys, other people's opinion of you tops your terror list. But you now know how to deal with them until your shyness is history. You know how to talk (or not) to people about it . . . even to yourself. You are able to work around tough situations and deal with shyness symptoms.

Now it's time to look at how other people *really* see you.

Nobody enjoys somebody telling them, "You've got it all wrong." But you are going to be thrilled when you realize "you've got it all wrong" about everyone's opinion of you, including your own.

Read on!

———•———

19

(6)

Can People Tell I'm Shy?

EVERYBODY'S LAUGHING AT ME

You probably imagine a bumper sticker on your forehead warning everyone "I have Social Anxiety Disorder" (as mental health professionals call shyness). So you think that they'll ridicule you or run. If you're like many Shys, every time someone looks at you, every time someone asks you a question, every time someone even smiles at you, it's an invitation to take it in the wrong way. Seriously!

Here is the thought pattern of most Shys:

Maybe they're just doing it to be nice to me because they know I'm shy.

Maybe they want to see how I'll react because I'm shy.

They probably don't like me because I'm shy and they're just trying to call attention to it.

Shys feel that everyone is judging them. Not true. Most people are oblivious to others' shyness. Guess what most people are thinking about? Right–*themselves.*

My father helped cure me of my shyness by telling me, when I was about fourteen, that actually everyone is normally so busy thinking about themselves and worried what you are thinking about them that they are not focusing on you nearly as much as you think. I saw it immediately. It is so mind-blowingly obvious once you see it.

–Pennant L., London, England

When your heart sounds like a repeater pistol in your chest, it's hard to believe that others can't hear it. Don't they see your face slowly beginning to resemble a sunburned lobster? But it's been proven beyond any reasonable doubt that most people have no idea that you're shy. In fact, chances are that they are shy, too.

About 13 percent of people in Western countries are lifetime Shys. Eighty percent say that they have had a shy period in their lives. And 40 percent say they are still anxious about themselves and the impression they're making.[3]

—ARCHIVES OF GENERAL PSYCHIATRY

THE GREAT PRETENDERS

Some Shys are able to put on a big show to cover their shyness. My shyness seminars often take place in a hotel where other seminars are scheduled at the same time. I sometimes see a few extremely outgoing people waiting to sign in for the program. They might be talking to others standing in line or joking with the registration person. In these cases, I go over to the "extroverts" and quietly ask if they are sure they are waiting for the right seminar. They usually give me a big smile and assure me that they are.

At first, I was confused but, as the seminars progressed, I discovered that many apparently confident people, or "Sures," as we're calling them, are excruciatingly shy and cover it well. No one would guess that these gregarious people suffer great inner turmoil. Outwardly confident people can be secretly self-conscious and constantly putting themselves down.[4] Even while they are laughing and chatting, they are painfully obsessed with what others think of them.

My shyness isn't what I would call "typical." I am thirty-two years old, and I come across as confident and friendly, the latter of which I am—not sure about the first. When I meet new people in a social gathering, for instance, I'll confidently say hello, but I tend to be self-conscious in ways that stifle my wish to strike up meaningful conversation. Strangers give me the creeps, but ask any of my friends and contemporaries and they'll say I am an up-front, go-for-it sort of guy. But inside I am a mushmallow. Keeping up the front is just so much work mentally (and I hate sweaty palms!).

—Michael D., London, England

Confidence-pretenders may look like they are enjoying themselves, but their suffering can be even more agonizing than for most Shys. Why? People often expect them to help with a project or attend an event, which, due to their shyness, they refuse. How many times can you come up with an excuse not to pitch in or party with friends? People start to mistrust or dislike the bogus Sures.

PEOPLE ARE CLUELESS

Tons of recent research confirms that neither Shys nor non-Shys can spot shyness accurately. Randomly picking one study out of the sociological hat, researchers looked for a group of people who had a fairly close association with each other. They chose forty-eight students who lived in the same college dorm.[5] These students chatted with each other in the dining hall and attended classes together. They saw each other around campus, studied together in the evenings, and even partied together on weekends. In other words, the inhabitants of this dorm knew each other *very* well.

First, the researchers sequestered each individual student to gather confidential information on how shy she or he really was. Once they had these data, they asked all of the students to secretly assess each of their dorm mate's degree of shyness.

The results astounded the researchers. They discovered that many of the shy students were judged *not shy* by 85 percent of their dorm mates. Conversely, some students who considered themselves to be exceptionally confident were dubbed *shy* by some of their colleagues.

You think that your shyness sticks out like a wart on your nose? No way. Ninety percent of the time, nobody can tell. And if by chance they do pick up on it, they don't dislike you for it. They're in your court and sorry that you're suffering from it. They, too, would like to see you emerge from your shell.

The next time you are chatting with people and a Shy Attack hits, realize that nobody notices it. Shyness is a 100 percent internal pain, like a stomachache from eating too much spicy food. Unless you're grabbing your stomach and groaning, nobody knows that your tummy feels like a train wreck.

ShyBuster #8
Tell Yourself "No One Knows I'm Shy"

And it's true. Unless you are shaking like a chicken on a caffeine buzz, no one will know you feel insecure. Repeat to yourself, "If 85 percent of people who *live together* can't tell if someone is shy, at least 99 percent of the people I meet can't, either."

---

⑦

Take Off Your Mud-Colored Glasses

When talking to someone, you try to hide your shyness. You struggle to keep good eye contact with her. But even if you succeed at these two challenges, it's tough to control your mind. You imagine that she thinks you're an idiot, that you bought your clothes at a garage sale, that you combed your hair with a rake this morning. You imagine her laughing at you inside, then gossiping to her friends about what a loser you are.

No! No! No! Pitch the paranoia and realize that is simply not true. Nine chances out of ten, she's not thinking about you at all. She's just babbling away, enjoying the sound of her own voice. On the slim chance that she is thinking about you, she's probably worrying what your opinion is of her!

Many dozens of studies have confirmed that Shys only *imagine* that people feel negatively toward them.

> Shy individuals imagine signs of disapproval or rejection that do
> not come from external stimuli but from long-term memory and
> internal cues. As such the individual's evaluation is not objective.
> It is prone to negative distortion or bias.[6]
> —*JOURNAL OF BEHAVIORAL RESEARCH THERAPY*

"I JUST KNOW THEY HATE ME"

How's this for an ingenious study proving it? Several researchers hired actors and a cameraman and bought some strange props. They then filmed the individual actors facing directly into the camera saying "hello" or "hi" as though they were meeting someone for the first time.[7]

The researchers directed one-third of the performers to project a warm, accepting "I like you" demeanor. They asked another third to give the camera completely neutral expressions as they pretended to be meeting someone. Then they told the last third to exude a chilly "You bore me—in fact, I don't like you" manner.

Of course, the resourceful researchers didn't want to depend entirely on the acting acumen of the thespians in the film. To assure scientific accuracy, they put a fragrant scent like a bouquet of flowers under the noses of the first group of actors to encourage an even more pleasant and accepting demeanor. Nothing was put in the vicinity of the noses of the "neutral expression" actors. The third group was filmed with an unspeakably revolting glop under their noses.

When the film was finished, the researchers showed it to a group of subjects, half of whom were confident and the other half of whom were shy. Both the Shys and the Sures were told to imagine that the performers in the film were meeting them personally for the first time. Pen or pencil in hand, the subjects gauged whether each actor in the film liked them or not.

The results? The Shys felt that most of the neutral faces were snubbing them. They even interpreted some of the warm expressions as social rejection. The only part the Shys got right were the performers who acted like they loathed them.

The dozen Sures, on the other hand, felt that most of the faces were positive toward them or neutral at worst.

The "jury" has reported. The verdict is in: *Most of the time, you are just imagining that people reject you.*

ShyBuster #9
Reject Imagined Rejection

The next time you meet someone and you think that they don't like you, realize that there is an overwhelming chance that you are dead wrong! It's your own imagination working overtime.

Like Sures do instinctively, consciously look at new acquaintances for signs of acceptance—their smiles, the warmth in their eyes, and their accepting body language. "Look and ye shall find."

8

Slay the Memory Monsters

HE SAID, SHE SAID

Have you ever had a painful social experience that you couldn't get out of your mind? Of course. All Shys have. That's one of our specialties. You go over and over what *he* said, what *you* said, then what *he* said again, then what *you* said . . . ad nauseam. Every time you run the scenario through your mind, it's worse than the last.

My best friend in boarding school, although exceedingly attractive, was an expert at that. In spite of her beauty, she was incredibly shy, just like me.

Our girls' school had a monthly mixer with a nearby boys' school. Of course, Stella and I always hung around the sidelines trying to look cool and disinterested. A lot of the girls were eyeing a really hot guy named Shawn. Over the summer, he had broken up with the most popular girl in our class—much to the delight of the school's entire female population.

At the first dance of the year, during our "who cares about boys" charade, Shawn smiled at Stella from across the room. He then came over and mimicked a deep bow. "May I have the pleasure of this dance, Madam?" Stella gulped.

Shawn must have noticed her reeling from the shock because he smiled, gently took her hand, and guided her to the dance floor. I ducked behind a pillar to spy on them.

During the dance, he noticed someone over her shoulder. Apologetically, Shawn excused himself. Stella's face dropped like a fallen soufflé. She quickly scurried over to me. "Leil, we are getting out of here."

"What?"

"Now! Right now!"

I Was So Boring

All the way back to the dorm, Stella was in misery. She whined, "I just knew he'd be turned off. I was boring him. He was just being kind to someone who looked lonely. He was just doing his good deed for the week, dancing with a dog to try to make her feel better. He probably already has a new girlfriend and didn't want her to see him dancing with anyone attractive. Maybe he. . . ." To Stella, the whole encounter was a disaster.

> Individuals with high levels of social anxiety often experience numerous highly intrusive and interfering thoughts about past unsatisfactory social events, which lead them to recall the events as more negative than they were.[8]
>
> –*Journal of Behavioral Research Therapy*

Several weeks later, we were scarfing down hot fudge sundaes at the counter of the local drugstore. Suddenly, Stella turned as white as a ghost and swiveled her stool toward me so that her back was to the door.

"Stella, what's the matter?"

"Shh. Keep your voice down. He just walked in."

"He who?! What he?"

"*Him*, Shawn–the guy who stranded me on the dance floor."

I looked over Stella's shoulder and, sure enough, Shawn was making a beeline toward Stella. As he came closer, he put his finger to his lips to signal me not to tell Stella.

Shawn gently tweaked her ponytail. "Hey, pretty girl, what happened to you at the party?"

Stella was speechless, so I filled in, "Uh, shortly after you left, we had to, uh, be somewhere by, uh, eight-thirty."

Shawn was surprised. "I didn't leave. I spotted a buddy giving me the fish eye because I owed him ten bucks, so I went over to pay him back and restore his faith in humanity."

He lowered his voice and smiled at Stella. "Then I went to the buffet table to get us both a snack. When I came back, you were gone." He put his hand on his heart and bent his head in mock despair.

I looked at my watch. "Oh my goodness, look at the time! I have to go now or I'll be late for my appointment," I lied.

"Uh, what appointment?" Stella stuttered.

Dummy! "Oh you know." But, of course, neither of us did.

A few hours later, Stella sailed into our dorm room and started dancing. She told me Shawn had asked her out for the following Saturday night.

DON'T BE A KILL-JOY (YOUR OWN!)

Unfortunately, Stella's happiness didn't last long. She and I were eating lunch with a girlfriend a few weeks after she'd met Shawn. Megan hadn't seen Stella since she started dating Shawn, so she was dying of curiosity. Despite heavy questioning, Stella insisted that she didn't remember how they met and finally snapped at Megan.

When we were back at the dorm, I asked Stella, "Why didn't you want to tell Megan about how you and Shawn met?"

"Leil, I told the truth. I really don't remember the details."

"Well, what *do* you remember?"

She thought for a minute. "Well, I remember that he left the dance before us."

Now I was relentless. "Why? Why do you think he left?"

"I dunno, I guess he was just bored and didn't want to dance with me anymore."

"Stella," I shouted, "Don't you remember the buddy he owed ten bucks to? Of course he liked you. He asked you out."

Stella rolled her eyes. "Yeah, but I don't know how long that will last."

My friend was hopeless. Like a typical Shy, she didn't even remember the pleasant parts, only the painful ones. Sadly, she would rerun it in her mind so often that she convinced herself that she acted badly. And that is the *only* part she'll ever remember.

> Individuals suffering from social phobia remember negative experiences longer than positive experiences.[9]
>
> –SOCIAL PHOBIA: CLINICAL AND RESEARCH PERSPECTIVES

IT WASN'T AS BAD AS YOU THINK IT WAS

The "negative perception" plot thickens. Not only do Shys fathom rejection when there is acceptance, they don't remember social situations accurately. Looking back, they see monsters that never existed.

> Shy subjects recall a pleasant social situation more negatively than it was.[10]
>
> –JOURNAL OF BEHAVIORAL RESEARCH AND THERAPY

It Starts Early

Even Shy toddlers have fuzzy negative recall of things. In a study called "Individual Differences in Children's Eyewitness Recall: The Influence of Intelligence and Shyness," teachers rated kids separately on intelligence and on shyness.[11] Then the children all went off to a birthday bash for one of their classmates. It was a real kid-pleaser: balloons, birthday cake, presents, singing "Happy Birthday"–the works.

A week later, researchers tested the kids to determine how much they remembered about the party. They asked each one: "What did the cake look like? What games did you play? Did you have a good time?" The researchers even threw in a few ringers, like "What happened when the poor clown dropped the ball?" But there had been neither a clown nor a ball at the party.

Clean Your Binoculars

The results: Intelligence had very little to do with the accuracy of the kids' recollections. The deciding factor was how confident they were. The self-assured kids remembered the events far more enjoyably and accurately than the Shy tykes. The Shys concentrated on negatives, especially those involving themselves. It's as though the Sure kids viewed the pleasant party through clear glass and the Shys saw it through a dirty mirror. Their own pessimistic self-image blocked the view.

> Subjects with Social Anxiety Disorder often forget or distort pleasant experiences.[12]
>
> –JOURNAL OF BEHAVIORAL RESEARCH THERAPY

That study could have added four words: "Even when they're kids."

Shy adults do the same. The more you think back on an event, the worse it gets in your memory. The best way to remember something accurately is to write it down before your cynical imagination gets carried away. That way, you'll have an objective account of what really happened.

ShyBuster #10
Be Your Own Social Scribe

Right after a social situation, write your *immediate* impressions. If you later remember anything negative about the encounter, go back and check your notes. If that embarrassing or disappointing moment isn't in your notes, *forget it*. It didn't happen.

(9)

Avoid Toxic People

IF YOU ACCEPT ME, I DON'T ACCEPT YOU

Groucho Marx, taking a puff of his pipe, said, "I don't want to belong to any club that will accept me as a member." Some Shys subconsciously agree with him–especially younger Shys who are still in school. They yearn to be part of a self-appointed "elite" group of students. When they are not welcomed, they feel something is wrong with them.

People who blatantly reject you are not worthy of your admiration. Don't try to break into their circle. You're just setting yourself up for a confidence game that you will lose.

A study called "Popularity, Friendship, and Emotional Adjustment During Early Adolescence" determined that disapproval, real or imagined, by anyone you admire colors your feelings toward yourself.[13] It's human nature. Kids in school form a pecking order just like chickens on a farm. If you ask any kid from the first grade up, "Who are the popular kids? And who are the unpopular kids?" they can answer like a knee-jerk reaction. Unfortunately, for many Shys, not being on the "preferred list" can deepen their self-doubt.

It's the same with adults who feel rejected (usually imagined) by more extroverted people in their club, church, or community.

Perhaps you admire someone's personality, clothing, choice of friends. So, if they don't choose you to pal around with, you think that they're slighting you because of your shortcomings. Such small things can color your entire view of yourself. And that imagined distorted color of yourself lasts a very long time, long after you've forgotten the names and faces of the people who you think didn't accept you.

I Only Want the Ones Who Don't Want Me

When it comes to women, men are especially susceptible to the "want the ones who don't want you" syndrome. Mr. Shy goes to a party and sets his sights on the best-looking woman there, a "ten" in attractiveness. For half of the party, he fantasizes about how he's going to make the approach. Finally he gets the courage to say "Hi!" She turns the other way.

Crash! His self-esteem craters. Mr. Shy slinks back to the bar feeling defeated and all the more shy.

Meanwhile, there is a lovely woman, a "seven," across the room who has been eyeing him all night. Think how terrific he'd feel about himself if he talked to her and she was obviously interested.

ShyBuster #11
Don't Choose Toxic Friends

Don't sabotage your self-esteem by trying to socialize with people who do not accept you openly. Instead, seek out people who respond warmly when you reach out to them. Don't wait for friends to come to you. Forge friendships with some people you really like or who might be in need of a friend themselves.

So what if this person you approach is not part of the "in crowd"? Just because certain people are "popular" does not mean that they are worthy of your esteem. Bill Gates was a reject from the cool crowd, but he didn't bemoan the fact that his more popular colleagues didn't accept him. The boys who put the first computer together in a garage weren't the "in crowd." Guess who got the last laugh?

Smart Shys Don't Play Stupid Games

Have you ever seen a play where the actor forgot his lines? How did you feel when that happened? Did you look down on him? Of course not. You were just uncomfortable for him.

That's the way some Sures feel around a Shy. They don't dislike you. They just feel *your* discomfort and don't know how to handle it. Additionally, some awkward or unsophisticated people think it "cramps their style."

Bantering and teasing is a trademark of the average American conversation, especially among younger or less cultured people. But Shys aren't used to putting other people down, even in fun.

Guys especially like to joke around with each other. "Are you always this stupid or are you making a special effort today?" Or, "I know you love nature–in spite of what it did to you. Ha ha!" They dish out an insult to a buddy and expect him to chew it up and spit back a witty putdown.

Of course, this foolish banter isn't just a guy thing. Women enjoy something similar. Rather than mocking each other, though, women often laugh about an absent colleague. Many years ago, Frank Sinatra called it "dishing the dirt with the girls." They're not malicious. They're just upholding the American teen stereotype.

CAN'T TAKE IT, CAN YA?

Teasing is not a pretty game, but it is fun for the insulters. It can be fun for the "insultees," too, but *only* if they know how to sling the slurs back. A tennis pro doesn't enjoy playing with a newbie who has never hit a ball. And there's no thrill in razzing somebody who can't spar.

It's hard when a group of people look like they're having fun and you're standing on the sidelines. You *think* that you'd like to banter with them. But with your more sensitive nature, you'd probably find it foolish. You don't feel inept because you're not a pro football player. So why feel inadequate that you don't play this combative game?

ShyBuster #12
Steer Clear of People
Who Make Fun of Each Other

Teasing is not a Shy's game. At the beginning of your struggle against shyness, you are probably too sensitive to let the bawdy insults "roll off your back." And most likely you don't enjoy insulting others either. The solution? Avoid these jokers.

If you're in a group and the conversation suddenly turns to a mocking match, don't storm or slink off sullenly. As long as it's not ethnic or salacious, laugh along with the rest of them. Then find an excuse to make a quick exit!

(11)

The Movie Called "Me"

If you were a filmmaker and shot the same motion picture twice with the same actors, costumes, set, and script–but from different angles–the two versions would be entirely different films. Likewise, a Sure sees a real-life situation very differently than you do. In fact, it would be hardly recognizable as the same scene. Your brain shoots situations from an extremely different perspective than a Sure.

Imagine that you are happily settled in your seat munching popcorn at the movies. You are captivated by the characters on the big screen. You pass judgment on which ones you like and which ones you don't like. You hope that the good guy gets the girl and the bad one gets the boot. You even form opinions about the supporting characters–he's a dupe, she's a doll, he's deep, she's shallow.

You aren't thinking about yourself. You don't obsess over what they think about you. You are observing *them*. You are comfortably inside your body looking out. Sociologists call this the *field perspective*.

To a great extent, this is the way Sures see the world. They reside securely in their own skins looking out at the "field." They form impressions about others and don't fret excessively about what other people think of them. Sures simply *assume* that they will be accepted.

Not so, the Shys. They automatically feel that people will reject them. When they remember an uncomfortable situation, many Shys mentally float outside their bodies and see themselves as they *supposed* other people saw them.

YOUR OUT-OF-BODY EXPERIENCE

In a strange sense, you *are* drifting around the room, observing yourself, judging yourself, criticizing yourself. You might think of it as an "out-of-body experience." Mental health professionals prefer the designation *observer perspective* because you are, in essence, observing yourself–usually with hypercritical eyes. However, when you feel entirely comfortable in a situation, you, too, view the world from the field perspective.

> People usually view situations from a "field perspective." Socially phobic individuals view situations from an "observer perspective." . . . Upon entering a social situation, socially phobic individuals form a mental representation of their external appearance and behavior as an audience might see them.[14]
>
> –*JOURNAL OF BEHAVIORAL RESEARCH THERAPY*

Think back to a recent experience where you felt confident. Perhaps it was at a summer picnic with your family. You are all seated at a wooden table in the woods, gobbling up hot dogs and guzzling pop. You watch your little nephew as he dribbles mustard down his chin. *What a messy kid*, you muse.

Your brother-in-law is sounding off about how hot dogs are made. You mumble to yourself, *He thinks he's the expert on everything. I wish he'd shut up.* You smell the dogs on the grill behind you. *Umm, smells good. I'd like another.* So you hop up and get one.

You are now in the field perspective. In other words, you are viewing the scene from *your* perspective, forming your own opinions.

However, if you were in a situation that made you tense–like a picnic with people you didn't know well–you might be thinking: *Everyone notices that I haven't said a word. They probably think I'm dense. I'm hungry. Should I ask to have another hot dog, or should I just go get one? No, I better not. They'll think I'm greedy. Besides, I'd probably spill mus-*

tard on my shorts and they'll think I'm clumsy. I don't think anyone here
likes me anyway.

The next time you start to think about the impression you are making, turn your mental camera around. Start consciously forming opinions about the other people rather than speculating about what they might be thinking about you. It's good practice to get you in the confident field perspective.

ShyBuster #13
Force Yourself to Observe Others

It's hard to go from nervous actor to confident filmmaker. But force yourself to consciously notice other people, what they're wearing, how confident they look, how they're reacting to situations and *other* people—not you.

Give yourself full permission to be "judgmental." Just like watching a movie, observe them and form opinions. Forcing yourself to ask "What do I think of them?" chases "What do they think of of me?" right out of your mind.

How to Handle a Past Bummer

GET REAL

"Thanks a bunch, Leil," you may be saying. "You've just told me that I'm seeing social situations through a muddy lens. Then you say that I remember them pessimistically and it gets worse each time I think of them! Then, to top it off, you're saying that I'll only remember the negative parts. Thanks for the bad news."

No, Shys, don't you see? It's good news. In fact, it's stupendous news! I have given you sociological proof that:

1. Shys imagine disapproval or rejection when it isn't there. (see Reference #6 on page 261)
2. Shys think they performed in past events far more negatively than they did. (Reference #10)
3. Shys distort or forget the good experiences. (Reference #12)
4. During a tense situation, Shys "watch" themselves from the outside like a disapproving audience. (Reference #14)

Why is all of this negative thinking good news? Because, it means that everything you did then and are doing now is better than you think. Although you can't go back and erase the pain your insecurity gave you, your expectations and interpretations of future situations can be altered. You will have more confidence in how you will act and react in the future.

ShyBuster #14
You're Better Than You Think You Are

Heed the studies. It's an open-and-shut case. People like you a lot more than you think they do. You performed a lot better in past situations than you think you did. Your rejection is greatly imagined.

Think of this the next time you face an intimidating situation. Repeat to yourself, "People like me more than I think they do." "I perform better in situations than I think I do." "And I only imagine rejection." Recalling these three proven points boosts your confidence as you face your next challenge.

The only bad news is that you didn't know how good your social life was. *You could have enjoyed it if you did!*

Your Three-Step Game Plan

Is there such a thing as a magic number? Maybe. From the Holy Trinity to the Three Stooges, the number three has always been special for me. And whenever I'm faced with a sticky situation, the solution comes to me, almost magically, in three parts. My war on Shyness was no different.

There are three fundamental principles that you must follow if you want to shed your shyness.

1. Avoid avoiding.
2. Construct your own personal Graduated Exposure Program. Everyone's is different.
3. And number three? Well, we'll save that for a surprise.

———•———

⑬

Hooked on Hide-and-Seek

The first biggie is a Shy's favorite game—avoidance. But, as you'll see, it's a risky one. It can become addictive. And the more you play it, the harder it is to quit.

Have you ever dodged anyone just to avoid making small talk? All Shys have. If I saw an acquaintance coming toward me, I'd cross the street and pray that he or she didn't see me. If a store were nearby, I'd dart into it until the coast was clear.

Some people say they've had an epiphany at the top of a Himalayan mountain or in a temple in India. Mine was walking along Main Street.

I was window-shopping one Saturday morning when I was a nursery school teacher. At one point, I spotted a fellow teacher strolling toward me. I found Mr. Fuller quite attractive, so the thought of chatting with him was terrifying. In a panic, I dashed into the doorway of the store I was passing.

I thought I was safe until I heard his voice behind me, "Miss Lowndes, what are you doing here?" I was trapped like a fly under a glass. I pivoted slowly to venture a weak hello, and, as I was turning, I saw what kind of business I'd taken refuge in. It was an XXX-rated boutique of "adult toys." When I finally mustered the courage to look at his face, Mr. Fuller was sporting an enormous grin.

He winked at me and said, "Was there anything in *particular* you were looking for, Miss Lowndes?" I bolted past him out the door, dashed down the street, and dove into a "respectable" store to sidestep him.

Needless to say, after that fiasco, I avoided him all the more. I never again made eye contact with Mr. Fuller. Whenever we passed in the hall, however, he'd say "Good morning, Miss Lowndes" in a voice that was curiously salacious for a second-grade teacher.

Hearing his snide voice filled me with fury–not against Mr. Fuller, but against my shyness. I declared war on it and was determined to win. I swore to myself that I would never again go out of my way to avoid "scary people."

My self-promise wasn't easy. Like an almost hopeless case, I suffered recidivism. I soon fell into my old pattern. If I saw a scary person coming, I'd pretend, even to myself, that I needed to buy something at whatever store I was passing. Each time I successfully dodged a person, I felt good. But only for a few minutes. I was fooling myself. In fact, I was making my condition worse.

GETTING A "KICK" OUT OF AVOIDING

It's not just athletes. Everyone has an intense physical reaction to winning. Victory is a fantastic feeling, almost like a "high." Unfortunately, shy individuals get a high out of successfully avoiding people who intimidate them.

When you evade someone, it is even more insidious than just psychological relief. It's not "just mental" any more than taking heroin is just mental. Avoidance is an addictive drug.

Whenever I avoided anyone on the street, it was a mental relief. I felt good because they didn't see me. I said to myself, "OK, I won't do it next time." But I always did.

–Dana N., Reno, Nevada

Right after an episode, you take a deep breath and say, *Whew, I escaped that one!* But it makes it all the harder because you crave that relief again and again. You dig a deeper rabbit hole that is harder to scurry out of each time. Like a junkie, you start to hate yourself for being so weak.

> For individuals with Socially Avoidant Personality, anxiety sub-sides following an avoidant response, thus reinforcing and esca-lating the avoidant response.[15]
>
> —*JOURNAL OF BEHAVIORAL RESEARCH THERAPY*

The solution? Start rehab immediately. Get the shyness monkey off your back. Quit dodging *all* small encounters.

Suppose that someone you know slightly is walking toward you. Don't pretend that you don't see him. Smile and say hi. Of course, it will feel uncomfortable at first because you are breaking your pattern. But I promise that you will be encouraged by his reaction. It will become easier and easier. When you see how warmly he responds, you will feel much better than you did when dodging him.

When walking in the street and someone is approaching from the front, it's a terrifying experience. What helps is simply to greet the person in passing—a simple smile, a nod of the head, and a "Hi" does wonders to break the awkwardness—and even builds a little confidence. (Wow, I said "Hi" and nothing bad happened, and he or she actually smiled back!)

—Koos V., Pretoria, South Africa

ShyBuster #15
Go Cold Turkey on Avoiding

The next time you spot an intimidating person and are tempted to pretend that you didn't see him or her, do not look away. Do not cross the street. Do not pull your hat down over your head. You're only making it worse for the next time. No matter how tough it is, put a big a smile on your face and say "hi." You've got nothing to lose, and everything to gain.

(14)

Shave Years Off Your Suffering

I'm sure many people have told you, "You'll just grow out of it." Are they right? Sort of. Think of it this way. Simply by living on this earth, you are gradually exposed to more and more situations as the years go by. And, naturally, you pick up social skills along the way. So, in a sense, they are right.

But do you really want to wait years to shed your shyness? Jump into the rest of your life today. With the help of *Good-Bye to Shy*, you can start your own professional program that has proven to be the most effective nonpharmacological treatment, bar none.

Mental health professionals call the process "Graduated Exposure Therapy." We'll call it "G.E.T" for short. Just one of the many dozens of studies proving that Graduated Exposure is the most effective cure puts it this way:

> Social Anxiety Disorder subjects receiving combination treatment of Graduated Exposure to fear-provoking situations and learning social skills improved significantly more on measures of community functioning than did subjects with any other treatments.[16]
>
> *–JOURNAL OF CONSULTING AND CLINICAL PSYCHOLOGY*

We've talked about the first crucial step on the path to confidence, *avoiding avoidance*. Now we come to the second: *Graduated Exposure*, gradually exposing yourself to increasingly scary situations. Pay attention! This is the biggie, the pulse of your Stamp Out Shyness campaign.

"FEARFUL PEOPLE ARE FREAKS"

In spite of all of the psychological and sociological proof to the contrary, some Shys still think that G.E.T. isn't really the way to get over shyness.

There are two reasons. One is that it's only natural to rationalize yourself out of something you don't want to do. And the second is that a few publicity-hungry, self-styled therapists have sensationalized Graduated Exposure. Here is a harmful example.

While channel surfing one day, I got caught up in an ugly wave. I happened on one of those television talk shows, or rather circuses, where people who suffer from an assortment of afflictions are on display. This particular program prefers people plagued with mental and/or physical disorders. The heartless host feigns compassion. He has an insatiable appetite for bizarre family relationships, strange sexual tastes, and other eccentric infirmities. While tearful guests bare their souls to millions of viewers, the studio audience hoots and hollers, egging them on to even more humiliation. In this particular installment, the guest had an unusual fear.

"Ralph is afraid of peaches," the host gleefully announced.

"Ooh," the audience chanted.

"He can't come near them."

"Ooh," the audience chanted louder. A basket of peaches appeared on a big screen behind Ralph. The host pointed up at it. Ralph turned, swore (bleeped out), screamed, and jumped up. Two hundred seventy pounds of sheer terror raced down the studio hall, followed, of course, by the camera crew.

Hysterical laughter from the audience.

Ralph, covered by three cameras, cowered in the corner backstage. At the host's goading, the audience began chanting, "Ralph, come back. Ralph, come back." Ralph, still shaking, staggered back on the set.

The crowd applauded.

While winking at the audience, the host asked Ralph, "Why don't you like peaches?"

"They're fuzzy, they're slimy." Then almost inaudibly, he muttered something about a girlfriend who had peach shampoo.

At that moment, two voluptuous women brought in two big baskets of peaches.

The audience's gleeful crescendo became "Uh-oh, he's in big trouble now!" At the sight of the peaches, the spectators were treated to a repeat performance from Ralph. This time he ran through the audience. They tackled him and succeeded in pulling his pants down. The camera caught the rear view of Ralph crawling away from the taunting audience on all fours, his trousers around his knees.

Ralph once again crouched in the fetal position in a corner of the studio wings. The host followed and sneered, "Do you know what you are now? A six-foot-tall, 270-pound man cowering in the corner!"

Mercifully for me, just then my phone rang.

Phobia Coach Cures Acrophobia to Zoophobia. Success Guaranteed. Walk-Ins Welcome.

When I came back fifteen minutes later, Ralph was happily holding a ripe peach in his hand. With a big smile, he brought it to his lips.

The camera cut to a self-described "phobia life coach and therapist" sitting paternally beside Ralph. He explained to a gullible audience that he cured Ralph by gradual exposure and that Ralph will never fear peaches again.

RIGHT IDEA, WRONG TIMING

Have you ever seen a nature film where a tiny flower bud bursts from the ground in a few seconds? Two seconds later, it sprouts leaves.

Another five seconds and exquisite petals open to receive the sunlight. The filming itself could have taken weeks. But we view this spectacle of nature in less than thirty seconds. If Ralph's host were an unethical horticulturalist rather than an emcee of debauched demonstrations, he would try to convince us that the flower buds actually blossomed in those few seconds.

For Ralph, it was the right idea, wrong timing. Gradually exposing someone to a feared object or situation definitely works–but not in an hour-long show.

> With successful exposure, social situations no longer cue danger-based interpretation and anxiety.[17]
>
> –*Journal of Behavioral Research Therapy*

EASY DOES IT

Dr. Bernardo Carducci, a highly respected therapist who has been researching shyness for twenty-five years, tells the story of Margaret, who was so petrified of spiders that she couldn't walk anywhere except on a wide cement sidewalk.[18] Her fear of spiders didn't permit her to enter any building but her own.

During treatment, the therapist first asked Margaret to simply write the word *spider* repeatedly. Her next task, probably weeks later, was to look at pictures of spiders in a book. It was a giant step, and probably a long time later, when she was able to view a spider in a glass box across the room. Ever so gradually, Margaret could come closer and closer to the little critter in the box. As her final victory, Margaret sat comfortably in a room with a spider crawling along the arm of her chair.

But this was no hour-long TV show. By the end of the first hour, Margaret was probably still trying to hold her pen steady while she wrote the word *spider*. Film coverage of Margaret's phobia and eventual cure would have made a rather humdrum TV show, lasting several months. But at least it would have been real.

The therapist had treated Margaret with Graduated Exposure Therapy–real Graduated Exposure Therapy, which takes a lot longer than forcing a peachaphobic to eat the fuzzy fruit in one sitting. *G.E.T. is* the *most effective nonpharmacological treatment for shyness and other phobias that exists today.*

> Gradual exposure guides patients to confront feared situations and allows their fear to dissipate naturally. They interpret it accurately and gain essential skills. Patients gain a sense of safety through not prematurely escaping from or avoiding social situations.[19]
>
> –SOCIAL ANXIETY DISORDER: RESEARCH AND PRACTICE

GET ON YOUR PRIVATE G.E.T.

The second "must do" to shed your shyness is to create a personalized program just for you taking into account your specific challenges. In essence, it is your own Gradual Exposure Therapy for people and situations that intimidate you. The easiest and the most difficult situations vary greatly for each individual Shy. What is a big challenge for one Shy may be a no-brainer for another.

One reason some Shys fail to shed their shyness is because they think that they have to force themselves to do very scary things right away. They feel that they need to accomplish the impossible, like winking at Mr. Wonderful today or asking Ms. Drop-dead Gorgeous for a date tomorrow. Or swaggering into the boss's office this afternoon and demanding a raise.

Therapists would call this technique "flooding."[20] But who wants to drown? Just dip your big toe in first.

How?

- **Past Jitters:** First, write a list of the people and situations that have made you uncomfortable in the past. For example, were you tongue-tied when someone asked you to "say a few words" to the group? Did you make a quick U-turn the minute you entered a party because everyone looked so intimidating? Did you avoid talking to an attractive someone?
- **Future Jitters:** When you've finished your list of past jitters, list some specific future qualms. Have you been asked to make a presentation to your team at work? Is there a menacing must-attend event coming up? Is there a special someone you'd like to spend more time with but are too anxiety-ridden to even talk to?
- **General Jitters:** Now write some broad-spectrum, general situations that make you shudder. They don't have to be ones you've confronted in the past or will have to face in the near future, just situations where even thinking about them makes your legs turn to linguine.

ShyBuster #16
Make a Jitters List

Compile a list of people and situations—past, future, and general—that make you feel like you have a wrecking ball in your chest and dripping sponges in your hands. Make it very specific, including even the names of the people who intimidate you.

Incidentally, you might be interested in how your hot spots compare to other Shys. Researchers polled patients suffering from Social

Anxiety Disorder on which situations they found most intimidating.[21] The three most menacing were meeting and talking with:

- Strangers, 70 percent
- Individuals of the opposite sex, 64 percent
- Authorities, 48 percent

Now shuffle your list around. Put the simplest challenge at the beginning and the most terrifying at the end. If you're somewhat comfortable talking to strangers at a cocktail party, but having a one-on-one dialogue at a dinner party makes you feel like you're sitting on broken glass, list the casual conversation of the cocktail party first and the dialogue of the dinner party after. Or it may be the reverse for you, in which case you would put dinner conversation first, cocktail parties next.

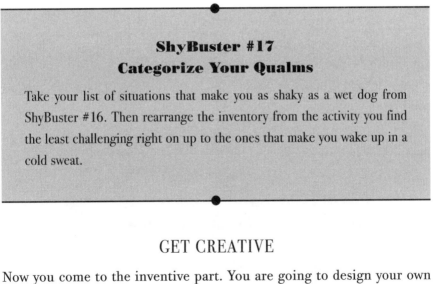

ShyBuster #17
Categorize Your Qualms

Take your list of situations that make you as shaky as a wet dog from ShyBuster #16. Then rearrange the inventory from the activity you find the least challenging right on up to the ones that make you wake up in a cold sweat.

GET CREATIVE

Now you come to the inventive part. You are going to design your own G.E.T. program. It is *the* proven way to conquer fear and shed shyness. Take the first challenge on your list and break the activity into small steps. Think of it as climbing a staircase where each step is higher than the last. You are building your muscles so that soon no step will be too high.

Suppose, for example, talking with people in authority terrifies you. Whenever you take the elevator at work, you live in fear that the CEO will step in. Now you're trapped. How do you act? What do you say?

Your staircase to a new comfort level might look something like this.

- **First step:** Chat with the supervisor of a different department. It's less scary than talking with someone who has direct authority over you.
- **Second step:** Chat with your own supervisor. This will be much easier after you've talked to the other supervisor. They're both on the same level.
- **Third step:** Chat with the department head. Sharing a few friendly words with him or her will feel more natural after conversations with the previous two authority figures.

Continue constructing your staircase until you feel that you could conversationally juggle an entire board of directors squashed together with you in the elevator.

ShyBuster #18
Construct Your Staircase of Doable Steps

Break each terrifying situation from your list in ShyBuster #17 into less scary smaller steps. Make sure each step is climbable. Even if you're feeling pretty confident and cocky about one step when you get to it, *don't skip it.* Just do it quickly before moving up. You build a more solid base when you follow your plan.

Your success may be slower or quicker than Margaret overcoming her "spider-phobia." But you won't have to sit down and write the word *party* one hundred times. Nor will I ask you to strut into a big bash tomorrow night. You will go at your own pace. But at least you know you're not swallowing snake oil.

THE *GOOD-BYE TO SHY* THEME SONG: "SIMPLE TO SCARY"

Just like Snow White's groupies sang "Whistle While You Work" to keep themselves happy on the job, you can hum the *Good-Bye to Shy* theme song to cheer you on to each new challenge. The lyrics are, "I'm starting with the simplest and working my way up to the scariest." You can put the song to your favorite music–classical, C&W, acid rock–as long as the lyrics are the same. Sing the song to yourself as you do every ShyBuster in the book.

Soon it will be tough to find *anyone* who intimidates you. You will be looking at, smiling at, and comfortably chatting with the scariest people–new acquaintances, the big boss, the movie star you run into, even the drop-dead fantastic potential partner who used to make you forget that your mother tongue was English.

Do the thing you fear most and the death of fear is certain.

–Mark Twain

The Wacky Confidence Warm-Up

YOUR SOLUTION TO THE ENERGY CRISIS

Now we come to the third secret ingredient to shed your shyness. It is a quality that everyone must have to "win" any big battle. It is a powerful force that goes by many names: passion, vigor, optimism, spunk, conviction, get-up-and-go, "oomph." In short, *energy*. You gotta have it to overcome any challenge. And, unfortunately, it's not usually a Shy's strong suit.

Being energetic is also an attractive quality. Researchers at the American Sociological Association scratched their scholarly heads and posed themselves a question: "What type of personality are people most drawn to?"

They quickly found the answer: Someone who is energetic and optimistic. Unfortunately, these are not the personality traits that immediately come to mind when you think of the word *shy*. In fact, research has shown that one of the most obvious personality differences between a Shy and a Sure is energy level.[22]

By energy, I don't mean jumping around like a wild pony or having a voice like a bullhorn. There is another kind of energy that people respect even more. It is a strong and quiet energy, yet one with a spirited internal life.

Whether you aspire to be a lively extrovert or to develop more internal confidence, the following exercise, as crazy as it sounds, will get you walking out the door in the morning with the energy you need to fight your battle against shyness. It will give you the air of confidence. And, as you'll see in the next section, when you look and act confident, guess what? Your mind begins to believe it, and you become confident.

IF IT LOOKS LIKE A SHY, SOUNDS LIKE A SHY, AND WALKS LIKE A SHY, IT MUST BE A SHY

Can you imagine a professional football player running onto the field without warming up? He'd get slaughtered in the first quarter. Without warming up, a ballerina would hobble home on a toe splint. And a singer, without warming up, would bust a vocal chord. Why should a Shy be any different? You must warm up before presenting the "Me" show to the world.

Let's take an average day: You wake up. You brush your teeth. You shower. You get dressed. You eat breakfast. As you walk out the door, a neighbor spots you. You utter a soft hello and quickly avert your eyes.

Hmm, he thinks, *If she looks like a Shy, sounds like a Shy, and acts like a Shy, she must be shy.*

Now let's change that scenario: You wake up. You brush your teeth. You shower. But this time, you don only your undies. Then you furtively look around your bedroom and lock the door. You close the window and pull down the shades so that the neighbors can't hear or see you.

Of course, you need to take precautions. If you live with others, perhaps your spouse, your roommate, or your kids, explain your bizarre behavior. And don't forget to familiarize the dog with your daily ritual so that it doesn't attack. Now . . .

WAKE UP LIKE A WACKO

Run around the room in your underwear and flap your arms like a demented duck.

Shout like a crazed football fan.

Jump up and down like a rabbit on speed.

Laugh like a lunatic.

Whirl around like a tornado.

Fall back on the bed, kick your legs high in the air, and shout at the top of your lungs, "Hoo ha, hoo ha, hoo ha! I'm making a fool of myself. And nobody cares!"

Ahem. Now stand up. Regain your poise. Smooth down your rumpled undies. Finish dressing. Comb your hair. Have a bite of breakfast. Kiss your spouse, your kids, or the dog good-bye. Now go out the door to greet the world with energy.

Oh, there's that nosy neighbor again. Since your body, face, and voice are warmed up and full of energy, it now feels natural to wave your arm, smile, and give a hearty "hello there."

Hmm, he thinks, *If she looks like a Sure, sounds like a Sure, and acts like a Sure, she must be sure of herself.*

ShyBuster #19
Do the Demented Duck Exercise

You think I'm kidding about this exercise? Absolutely not! Act like a demented duck on speed in the morning. Get loony. Get loud. Get unglued . . . from shyness. Explode your energy sky-high in the morning, then let it settle gradually. It works a lot better than trying to haul it up out of a hole.

Naked Dancing Anyone?

When you get really good at the wacky energy exercise, you can start your day by dancing naked in front of the mirror. Then try to act shy!

PART

4

The Seven Best Beginner's ShyBusters

Those of you who have read my other books know one of my most deeply held beliefs. In fact, for me, it has reached the highly elevated state of an ideology, a dogma, a tenet, gospel. It is (trumpet blare, please): *Fake it 'til you make it.*

At first glance, that seems like lightweight advice, the kind you'd find promulgated in *Cosmo* or some of the less profound newsstand publications. But it is wisdom for the ages.

Mother Nature created it. Ancient philosophers expounded on it. Gestalt principles confirmed it. And recently it has been carved in stone for the modern world–in more erudite words, of course–by a research team with a grant from the Behavioral Science Division of the Ford Foundation.[23] Now that you've got your act together, it's time to raise the curtain on a confident-looking new you. You're going to *fake confidence 'til you are confident.*

———— • ————

(16)

It's Show Time!

The old chestnut, "You never have a second chance to make a good first impression" is splendid news for Shys. So is another, "First impressions last practically forever." That means, if you pump it up and put pizzazz into your personality for a paltry ten seconds when greeting someone, that memory takes a long time to fade.

Why ten seconds? That is the time it takes to make a first impression. Even the most lethargic librarian can juice it up for that amount of time.

GIVE YOURSELF AN OCCASIONAL "ZAP"

If you've faithfully been doing your daily demented duck exercise, you know how it feels to have high-octane energy flowing through your veins. But there is no need to maintain that super-cheerful, gung-ho personality all day. It would come across as fake, and you'd have to be carried home on a stretcher. There are, however, a few strategic moments throughout the day when you should recapture that energy.

One of them is arriving at work. Just before entering the door, throw your shoulders back, soften your face into a relaxed smile, and give a lively greeting to anyone you know. This certifies you as part of that most beloved species, human beings who are energetic and optimistic.

You don't need to stay chipper and revved up all day. After that first little burst of effervescence, your coworkers will see you as a confident and congenial individual whose quietness means that you're concentrating on your work.

I'm basically a very quiet person and don't have much to say in a group. I work in a post office, and a woman there gives everybody a big "hello" every morning. People like her a lot, so I thought I'd try it. I think my coworkers were surprised the first time I did it. I stayed with it, however, and I see people responding to me better, although I'm just as quiet as I used to be after my big hello.

—Tina G., Concord, New Hampshire

"HAPPY TO MEET YOU. I JUST WON THE LOTTERY!"

The energy burst is especially important when you are meeting someone for the first time. Let's say that someone introduces you to Archibald at a Chamber of Commerce meeting. "Hello, Archibald, I'm so happy to meet you," are the words. But you say them as though you had just won the lottery. Now that Archibald has pegged you as Mr. or Ms. Personality, he will interpret any ensuing silence as your being a good listener.

You will find many occasions to repump the wacko energy juice through your veins for a few seconds—passing someone in the hall, answering the phone, responding to a question, greeting an acquaintance, complimenting a stranger. In each case, those ten-second blasts of animation can lead to long-term benefits.

ShyBuster #20
Detonate Ten-Second "Blasts of Animation"

Sure it's tough. But how bad can being animated for ten seconds be? Light your internal sparkler in short bursts at appropriate moments, and you will see the spark spread like wildfire. As you see people warming up, you will instinctively light it again and again. You can become as much of a fireball of energy as you wish.

So Who's the Boss Here, Your Mind or Your Body?

THE MIND-BODY BATTLE TO BE TOGETHER

Your mind and your body instinctively strive to be in accord with each other. If they are not, you feel unbalanced.

When your mind thinks *I am shy*, your body accommodates and acts shy. And when your body moves like it's shy, your mind says, *I guess I'm shy*.

Here are your mind and body having one of their daily chats:

Mind: Hey, Bod, why are we slumping? What are you trying to tell me?

Body: I'm telling you, Brain, that we are shy.

Mind: Well, there certainly is a lot of physical evidence. I guess you're right, Bod. We are shy.

Body: Excuse me, Brain. Did I just hear you say we are shy?

Mind: Well, yes, Bod. Observe how we slump and can't look people in the eyes.

Body: Um, I guess you're right, Brain. OK, I'll accommodate you and move like a Shy. Maybe I'll even add a little blushing and stuttering to be more convincing.

Mind and Body (in unison): Wonderful, then we'll be together again.

In a bizarre sort of way, that satisfies you. Your mind and body agree. The mental health community calls it "cognitive consistency," and human beings instinctively strive for it.

So how do you escape this Catch-22? You have two choices. The first choice is to convince your mind that you are not shy so that your body behaves accordingly. This takes a long time on the psychiatrist's couch, lots of money, and maybe some pharmacology thrown in.

Your second option is to train your body to act confidently so that your mind follows suit. This is what the experts recommend. It's a lot easier to whip your body into shape than your brain. You know all the basic stuff: Stand tall, look people in the eyes, smile, and speak up. Then the new conversation goes like this:

Body: Hey, Mind, let's go to the party.

Mind: Yahoo! I'm ready. You're lookin' pretty good. Let's go party!

I read somewhere that a negative mind-set causes negative body language, but that the opposite is true, too—you can alter your attitude by adopting a positive demeanor. I tried that, by at first simply forcing myself to walk upright and hold my head level—while still avoiding others' gazes. That did boost my confidence to a point where I could start looking at people, then later on make and hold brief eye contact, to the current point where about half of the people I make eye contact with break it first.

–Koos V., Pretoria, South Africa

WHAT SUPER SURE LOOKS LIKE

A multitude of fascinating factors come under the "looking confident" umbrella. There isn't space here to explore the thousands of subtle signs that signal confidence. (I cover them in my book *How to Talk to Anyone: 92 Little Tricks for Big Success in Relationships*.) However, here are a few hints about body movements that self-assured VIPs do instinctively to get you started.

- When you are at a gathering, do not stand close to the wall or by the snacks. Walk directly to the dead center of the room. That's the place where all of the important people gravitate.
- When you are going through a large door or open double doors, don't walk on one side. March straight through the middle. It signifies confidence.
- At a restaurant, unless there is an established hierarchy, go for the seat at the end of the table facing the door. That is the power position.
- Sit in the highest chair in a meeting or on the arm of the couch–but not higher than the boss!
- Make larger, fluid movements. Confident people's bodies occupy more space. Shys take as little space as possible, as if to say, "Excuse me for taking up this much of the earth."
- Keep your hands away from your face. Never fidget.
- When you agree with someone, nod your head *up* from neutral (jaw parallel to the floor), not down.
- When passing someone, be the last to break eye contact.
- For men: Don't strut like a bantam rooster. But to look like a leader, swing your arms more significantly when you walk. When you are seated, put one arm up on the back of a chair.
- For women: To seem self-assured, square your body toward the person you're talking to and stand a tad closer. Naturally, give a big smile, but let it come ever-so-slightly slower. That way it looks sincere, not nervous.
- And, of course, need I even mention posture?

Practice these moves consciously until they become second nature. When you move like a Sure all day long, your mind becomes convinced that you already are one.

ShyBuster #21
Take the "Master's Position"

Whenever you catch yourself in that "Beat me again, Master" body language, snap out of it. Throw your shoulders back. Stand in the middle of the room. Sit in the highest seat. Take the "power position" at a table. Walk through the middle of a door. Don't fidget. Make large, fluid movements—the signs of confidence go on and on. Train your body to do these moves until they become second nature.

(18)

Eye Contact Made Easy

"**M**ake more eye contact." For Shys, that's like commanding a vampire to make good eye contact with the sun. *What if he wants to stop and talk to me? What if I freeze up? What if she thinks I'm stupid? What if he sees me blushing? What if . . . ? Well, I'll just pretend I didn't see him.*

Sound familiar? Your eyes are a vital body part of your Stamping Out Shyness campaign.

Some well-meaning people advise, "Look at people's eyebrows." (Do they really believe you can have a meaningful conversation with a pair of eyebrows?) Or, "Look at the bridge of their nose." (Sure, then they tell their friends you're cross-eyed). Tricks don't work.

There is no way around it. Shys *must* master good eye contact.

If only we thought like the Asians. To them, having little eye contact is a sign of respect. Alas, we can't inject their mores into our customs and polish our shoes with our eyes while talking to the boss. Here in the land of the brave and the free, we must have eye contact commensurate with our culture–confident, courageous, dominant, risk taking, and pioneering. Unfortunately, when you avert your eyes, these are not qualities you exude. Poor eye contact can be misinterpreted as shifty, shy, sneaky, snobbish, or untrustworthy. That in itself makes it worth majoring in eye contact.

BABY, WHAT BEAUTIFUL EYES YOU HAVE

I never cease to be amazed by babies' eye contact. Their tiny fearless eyes stare straight into mine. They look confident. When they grab their little toes and squeal with delight, they aren't wondering whether their feet are too big or too small. If I should gently poke their little tummies, they don't think I mean, "Getting a little tummy there, aren't you?" They don't blame themselves for scarfing down that extra jar of puréed applesauce and peaches.

Babies think that they're pretty cool no matter what they look like. And they assume that everyone else thinks they are, too. So they confidently keep gazing at me until they get bored. "Ho hum," they decide. "Now I'll stare at some other silly adult face."

Conversely, of course, no matter how shy you are, you wouldn't be intimidated by looking into a baby's eyes. Thus, a great place to start becoming comfortable with lingering eye contact is to stare right back into a baby's eyes–just the way he or she gawks at you. Eyes are eyes, whether they are six months old or sixty years old. Once you get used to tiny eyelashes, pupils, and irises, you'll feel more relaxed looking into those of teenagers. You can graduate to adults' eyes, authority figures' eyes–and then drop-dead gorgeous eyes.

ShyBuster #22
Peer into Infants' Eyes

If you have a major problem making eye contact with people (and what Shy doesn't?), start taking baby steps. Gaze into an infant's eyes. Babies' tiny peepers will start you on your way. Of course, "staring down a baby" isn't quite like staring down a charging bull. However, strong eye contact with the under-two set familiarizes you with the crucial "eyeball-to-eyeball" game. Incidentally, don't stare too long at little kids, or their mothers will call 911.

Work Your Way Up the Eyeball Chain

Once looking into a baby's eyes is no sweat, work your way up the scale to tots, then preteens, then teens. Don't stop there. After you have mastered making eye contact with juvenile eyes, gradually graduate to good eye contact with people your own age. You may be able to make a smooth transition. If, however, you find yourself simply unable to keep eye contact with people of a particular age group, there is an intermediary step.

JUMP TO THE GERIATRIC SET

When you reach the point where even slightly younger eyeballs make you jittery, skip them for the moment and shimmy to the top of the totem pole. Look into seniors' eyes.

Start with the over-seventy set—sitting on a bus, waiting in line, wherever and everywhere. Many elderly people, especially in large cities, feel neglected. Look right into their eyes, smile, and make them feel special. You'll be doing both of you a favor.

In high school, I couldn't look a single person in the eye. In class I kept to myself and during breaks I would escape to the back of the school's hall. Interaction with my peers virtually "paralyzed" me with fear.

Interestingly enough, I have little problem interacting with people much younger or older than I am—I am not too shy around kids or people approximately the age of my parents. But the closer someone gets to my own age, the more intimidating they are to be around.

–Scott S., Watertown, South Dakota

GO FOR EAGER EYES

Now let's raise the bar on beginner's eye contact. As soon as you've completed the "Young Eyes/Old Eyes" exercises, take on some anonymous eyes. These are people who are just waiting for your eye contact.

For example, salespeople, standing behind their counters in a department store, have been told to smile at customers. Help them do their job! They are eager for your eye contact. Rather than eyeballing strangers on a crowded street who are not just waiting for the moment you grace them with your smile, try catching the eye of the cosmetic clerk or the shoe salesperson.

You asked for "success stories" with shyness. I had a terrible time smiling and making eye contact with people. So I started making eye contact with people who didn't intimidate me. I looked at bus drivers when I got on the bus, cashiers when I bought something, and waitresses when they served me something. The more I got used to that, the more I was able to make eye contact with other people and people I knew.

—Ken K., Beaver Falls, Pennsylvania

ShyBuster #24
Go for People Who Want Your Eyeballs

Walk through a department store and make brief eye contact with every salesperson. They are eager for your smile and glance. Women, when you feel comfortable, stroll through the men's department and make eye contact with the salesmen there. Men, when you can make eye contact with the cosmetics clerks, you'll know you've graduated from beginners' eye contact.

As in all *Good-Bye to Shy* exercises, monitoring never hurts. If you have a friend who knows you're shy, take her shopping with you. Make a deal. If you don't meet your target number of eye-contact "hits," you buy your friend lunch.

(19)

The Clinically Proven Cure for "No Eye Contact"

Later on, I'll tell you about my great epiphany on the potty that told me to take a "people job" for a while. I chose to become a flight attendant with Pan Am, the now-defunct airline. The following ShyBuster was introduced to me by one of my coworkers—now a lifelong friend.

It all started on an overseas flight just after we finished serving dinner to 200 passengers. Back in the galley, wiping roast beef off our uniforms, she sensitively asked if I was shy because she noticed that I hadn't made much eye contact with the passengers. I liked her gentle approach and said yes. We talked a lot that flight, and, by the time the sun was streaming in the plane windows, we knew we'd be good friends.

DR. DAFFY DID IT

Daphnis (Daffy, for short) shared an apartment with her brother in Astoria, New York, known as "Little Greece." While visiting her once between flights, she said, "Leil, I think I have a cure for your problem with eye contact."

"Oh, good." *Here comes another flop*, I thought. "Really? Tell me."

"I want you to look directly into my eyes, and I'll look into yours. We'll see how long we can hold it."

We tried, but I broke up laughing each time.

"Leil, stop it. I'm deadly serious about this." She stood up in exasperation. "Go ahead and enjoy being shy for the rest of your life. See if I care."

That convinced me. After half a dozen feeble attempts, I was able to gaze directly into her eyeballs for about thirty seconds and feel completely at ease.

"Wow, how did you learn that exercise, Daffy?"

"In school. We were studying how important eye contact is. One afternoon, the professor asked us to sit next to somebody we didn't know and look intently into each other's eyes. Most of us cracked up. But all week he made us change partners and stare longer and longer until we could do it for a full minute. Then he asked us to carry on a conversation with each other and not break eye contact even for a second.

"Leil, the results were unbelievable. When we discussed it Monday morning, everyone reported they'd had more contact with everybody they'd talked to over the weekend."

> In the Netherlands, VVM, the Association of Shy people founded in 1988, has been extremely effective with people who are profoundly shy. During their training, all members must look someone in the eyes for graduating amounts of time. These exercises have been found to also help problems with blushing and not taking the initiative (in conversing).[24]
>
> —*WORLD PRESS REVIEW*

"Yeah, but you're a friend, Daf. I don't think I could do it with a stranger."

She smiled, "Let's see." Her brother Nicias, whom I had never met, was upstairs studying. Daffy called him from the staircase, "Nicky, could you come down and help us with something?"

When I looked up to say hello, my heart leapt up to my throat. Nicias was nothing short of a Greek god. Daffy explained what we had been doing and asked him to take her place in the "eye contact game." It would have been difficult enough to gaze into the eyes of a "normal" person, but with Adonis, it seemed impossible! For Shys, the more desirable someone is, the harder it is to look at them.

When she said "Go," our eyes locked. A blush spread over my face like wildfire, and my heart felt like a jackhammer. I forced my eyes to stay on his. Slowly, very slowly, the fire simmered down and the jackhammer switched into low gear.

When Daffy gauged that my vital signs were returning to normal, she said, "OK, time's up." Nicias went back up to study. I threw my arm up to my forehead, "I cannot bee-lieve what I just did, Daffy!"

ShyBuster #25
Glue Your Eyeballs to a Buddy's

Assure a close friend or relative that you haven't gone bonkers. Then ask for his or her help with the staring exercise. Look steadily into each others' eyes for longer and longer periods of time. When you've worked your way up to a minute, have a conversation with your friend while maintaining exaggerated eye contact.

I promise that the next time you are speaking with a stranger, it won't feel like you are looking a charging bull in the eyes.

By repeating this exercise, eye contact (which you now feel is exaggerated) will soon feel natural. Direct eye contact for a Shy is like staring down a gun barrel. But keep at it and soon you won't even think about it.

I guess subconsciously I realized that if I survived looking into the hottest, most beautiful eyes I'd seen all year for a full minute, how bad could a few seconds with "normal" eyes be?

THE UNSPOKEN "I LIKE YOU"

Why is it that just a split second seems like an eternity when you're making eye contact with strangers or intimidating people? It's like the slow-motion movie action when someone is in an auto accident or is punched. Somebody slugs the good guy. The sound track goes silent and the scene slows down. His head slowly revolves to the side from the impact. His body falls at a snail's pace to the floor.

That's how eye contact feels to a Shy. Those few seconds can feel like an hour.

I try to smile and make eye contact with everyone because I know I should. But it is so painful to keep my eyes on someone else's. And sometimes I feel like I'm smiling at them like a hyena. My mind is racing a mile a minute and the temptation to finish my smile and look away is too big for me to resist. Once I tried counting to three, but it seemed so long. I don't want people to think I'm staring at them. But if I stop smiling and looking at them, they think I'm unfriendly.

–Claire M., Bloomfield, Vermont

Claire's concept of counting to three while looking someone in the eyes is good. However, repeating dull numbers can still seem interminably long. Furthermore, counting doesn't give you a warm expression or smile, which are crucial to effective eye contact.

Try this technique: When greeting someone, look at their eyes and *silently* say, "I like you" to your eye-contact recipient. There are three advantages.

1. The time it takes for you to say to yourself, "I like you" is precisely the amount of time lingering eye contact should last.
2. Saying those words silently gives you a warm expression. Unless you really work at it, your mind can't say "I like you" and your face say "I'm scared stiff" at the same time.
3. Your inner monologue keeps your mind from racing to other thoughts–like "I wonder what they think of me."

ShyBuster #26
Say "I Like You" Silently During Eye Contact

While keeping eye contact with someone, silently say to yourself, "I like you." Now you're right on target with timing for your eye contact and smile. Soon it will become second nature, and you can chuck this crutch.

20

A Quick Smile and a Slow Jet Get You Nowhere Fast

Eye contact without a slower smile is like a crackle without a pop. It has no effect at all. You can't just flash your teeth at someone and think you're done.

How your smile feels from inside your cheeks can be very different from the smile other people see. You *feel* like it's as wide as a watermelon. But to recipients it can look like a dill pickle.

The slow-motion phenomenon comes into play here, too. You think you're smiling interminably long. But in actuality, it can be so quick that they'll miss it if they blink.

IS THE SMILE YOU GIVE THE SMILE THEY GET?

Maybe you've become successful at giving longer smiles to people. However, you feel as though your smiles are forced and unnatural. I have received many e-mails from people who said they'd tried to smile but didn't get much response from people. Could they be suffering from what I now call "Stephen's Syndrome"? He wrote . . .

I didn't date very much, but I had some good friends in college. When I moved to Boston for my first job, I was lonely and wanted to meet some women. I'd go to bars and clubs and smile at some attractive women, but they'd never smile back. So I never dated much there, either.

Then I got transferred to Los Angeles. I love California. It's much more friendly than Boston for me. Women actually ask me to dance with them. I started going regularly to a club in Long Beach. One night, a woman I was dancing with asked me what I always looked so sad about. I was surprised and asked her if I looked sad. She said she'd been watching me for several weeks at the club and I always looked sad. I remembered that several other people had told me that over the years, too. I decided to try to look happier, because maybe I looked sad even when I wasn't.

–Stephen S., Los Angeles, California

I never met Stephen, but it sounds as though he *thought* he was smiling. However, women didn't see it that way.

To remedy the situation, all you need is a well-lit mirror, say the bathroom mirror. A sense of humor definitely helps, too. Lock the bathroom door lest your family see you grimacing like a monkey on a banana boat. Now, look at yourself and smile big. Smile small. Smile sexy. Smile sad. Smile sarcastic. Smile salacious. Smile scared.

Then top it off with a pretentious smile and a phony smile. Why? You need to know how even the nasty ones feel *from the inside*. That way you don't run the risk of flashing one of those creepy smiles when you mean it to be friendly.

ShyBuster #27
Make Faces at Yourself in the Mirror

Get to know your smile, from the inside, from the outside, from the right and left. Feel the difference between grinning and grimacing. Know when you are leering like a lecher or smirking like a stalker. Only when you know how each feels can you polish yours to a confident, friendly, and welcoming smile. You'll know you've succeeded when you see your eyes getting into the act.

SMILE AT WHAT'S INSIDE

Once again, practice from simplest to scariest, just like with your eye contact. Start smiling at your cat, your dog, your goldfish, and babies. As with eye contact, you can then jump to smiling at that sweet little elderly lady on the bus or the old codger who lives down the street. Not only are these "beginner smiles" crucial in your antishyness campaign, but they give joy to everyone you smile at.

Realize that inside every wrinkled old lady lurks a beautiful young girl. Inside every tattered old man lives a college football star. When you smile at them, they feel like you're smiling at their inner selves. It's a win-win situation.

ShyBuster #28
Smile at Their "Inner Selves"

Lest this sound too touchy-feely, let me explain. Search for something special, funny, or nice about everyone who comes into your line of sight. Concentrate on that and a smile comes up from your gut, naturally. Find *any* excuse to smile! Does the lady in the bank line have a cute little kid? Smile at her. Did the driver of the car next to yours sneeze? Smile at him. Did someone smile at you? Make *sure* you smile back! Like any exercise the more you do it, the easier—and better—it gets.

In fact, make a game of it. Count the number of smiles you are able to give in a day. Then try to top your quota the next day.

MAKE YOUR SMILE A REALITY SHOW

Now it's time to make your smile a "reality show"—smiling at people you know. First smile at people you don't find threatening, like the intern who works at your company. Work your way up to those who intimidate you slightly, say a colleague at work or a nice-looking person whom you're not personally attracted to. Then your supervisor. Then your supervisor's supervisor. You get the idea. Keep smiling at scarier and scarier people.

Snobs Don't Smile

We know how people catch chicken pox, what they feel like, how long they last, and how to treat them. Nobody is going to look at a face full of red speckles and say, "What in the world are those funny red spots?"

Shyness isn't so conspicuous. People don't know that you're dizzy, nauseous, numb, and sweating like a hog in a sauna. But they can think something worse. If you don't make eye contact and smile, they often misread shyness and interpret it as snobbery.[25]

Some people think of shy people as unfriendly or as snobs. This is not true. It is a very bad misunderstanding because most of us shy people care very much about other people. In my case, it is because I am often so worried that what I say might be misinterpreted or that it would hurt somebody.

–Wendy T., Little Falls, Minnesota

"WHO, ME? A SNOB?"

Think about it. Snobs don't acknowledge people first. Shys don't, either. Snobs don't greet people with their names. Shys don't, either. Snobs don't hang out with the gang. Shys don't, either. So is it any wonder people might mistake a Shy for a Snob?

If I'd known that in college, it would have saved me sleepless nights. In junior year, I had an all-consuming crush on a sexy guy in my Art class. He was French–from Paris, yet. I envisioned Jacques riding on a bicycle wearing a beret with a long baguette under his arm. I pictured us kissing under the Pont-Neuf on the banks of the river Seine. (Somehow kissing under Garrison Avenue Bridge over the Arkansas River didn't hold the same glamour for me.)

I loved the way he spoke. Ever since I was a teenybopper, foreign accents have made my knees go weak. (I didn't know at the time that accents are just badly pronounced English.) But, alas, all I could do was sneak shy, surreptitious peeks at Jacques from behind my easel.

Right after Art, we both had Chemistry on the other side of the campus. The instant the bell rang, I'd swiftly stash my brushes and sprint across the campus. I was terrified that, if we walked together, I'd be speechless or say something stupid.

Once, during my usual breathless sprint, I heard footsteps running behind me, then a throaty French accent.

"Lili, Lili! Lili, why ees it you are walking zo fast?"

I froze like a frightened ferret. Words felt like wood shavings on my sandpaper tongue.

Jacques caught up with me and asked, "Lili, we both go zees way every day, but you never walk with me. You do not like me?"

"Uh, no. No no, I mean yes."

"Voilà, it is settled then," he said with feigned bravado. "From today on, ve vill walk together to Chemistry class. Yes?" My heart was beating so fast, he must surely have heard the thumping. We strolled a few seconds in silence, him smiling and me screaming inside. Finally, I was unable to halt the tears welling up in my eyes.

"Lili, ees somezing wrong?" he asked.

I could hold it back no longer. I blurted out, "I am shy!"

"Excuse me, you zaid you are what?"

"Shy! Shy!" I sobbed.

He put his hand on my shoulder. "Lili, I am zo happy now because I felt you were avoiding me because you did not like me. Excuse me for saying, but I thought you might be what you Americans call a snub."

"A snub?" I managed to croak.

He laughed. "Oh, no, I mean a snob."

I couldn't believe it. Jacques thought I was stuck-up!

IT'S FOR THEM, NOT YOU

Shys, because you are often more sensitive than Sures, you especially don't want to hurt others by acting as though you are slighting them. For years, you have been screaming at yourself, "Don't act shy!" Your main reason, of course, is because it is so agonizing for you.

Turn the lens around. Think of it from others' viewpoints. Change your inner dialogue. Tell yourself, "I must smile at people, for *their* sake, not mine. If I don't, they might think I'm ignoring and rejecting them."

My worst year was my first year in high school. I was shy to the point where I couldn't look anybody in the eyes. I always avoided looking at faces by looking down. So much so that I sometimes walked past my classmates without realizing it, because I was too afraid to look up. They thought I was snubbing them so I wound up not having any friends.

—Sonja P., Seattle, Washington

COMPLIMENTS SHOW CONFIDENCE

If large, lingering, and sincere smiles are still a challenge for you, reinforce them. How? The simplest and most effective way is to give others a sincere compliment. Truly search for something you like about them. That's a "lovely necklace," "a terrific shirt," "a beautiful color on you." There are hundreds of etceteras. Your praise signals them that you are not a snob.

GOOD LOOKS CAN COUNT AGAINST A SHY!

Good-looking Shys, you are much more at risk for people thinking you are arrogant. After all, they figure, if you are so stunning, the world is your oyster. Why should you even look at them?

I suffered a great deal of misunderstanding when I was in college. I was blessed with good looks, and many people mistook my timidity for overbearing arrogance and were insulted by it. The worst part was that I actually knew this and tried to turn my image around. But I was terror stricken to speak to anyone. One time I overheard one of the girls whispering to another as I walked by that I was stuck-up and thought I was better than everybody else. Nothing was further from the truth.

　　　　　　　　　　　　　　　　　　–Darlene N., Los Angeles, California

Remember, Good Looking, you are much more at risk for being misunderstood than the rest of us mortals. Therefore, you have to double your efforts to be friendly and greet everyone.

If at First You Don't Succeed, Swear!

THREE STRIKES AND YOU'RE *NOT* OUT

If you don't succeed at first with the previous ShyBusters, swear to keep at it. None of them are impossible. Make a solemn promise to yourself that you will try again and again until you succeed. I learned that lesson early, but I wish I'd kept it up. I would have shed my shyness years earlier if I had.

When I was twelve, I was a phone-a-phobe. Big time! I would shudder and turn the other way when passing the telephone. It was ominous and the cord looked like a coiled, poisonous black snake.

Whenever the phone rang, I'd run from it. The bathroom was my customary hideout. Sometimes I'd jump into the empty bathtub, pretending to be taking a bath. Even then, I realized how pathetic it was, a twelve-year-old girl crouching in the tub fully clothed and shivering like a sick kitten.

Every night, I prayed, "Please, dear God, don't make me afraid of the telephone anymore." After my prayer one night, I dreamed I was cowering in the empty tub again. Suddenly the bathroom walls trembled. As though there were a speaker in every tile, I heard a deep voice in Dolby surround sound: "My child, I only help those who help themselves." I woke up in a cold sweat and resolved to conquer the beast.

The next morning, I descended the staircase feeling like a saint following God's divine calling. I dialed the first seven digits that came to mind, but quickly hung up.

I tried again. Ring . . . I hung up.

I tried again. Ring . . . Ring . . . Ring . . .

No one home. I breathed a sigh of relief and walked away feeling that I had succeeded.

In fact, I had! Even though I hadn't completed one call, I was on the right track. Unfortunately, many Shys don't look at it that way. Early failure is not a confirmation that you can't do it. Do not crawl back into your shell and feel like you are destined to dwell there forever. Success only comes to those who persist.

When I was a kid we lived in Florida. I didn't have any friends because I was too shy. But there were lots of flat streets and I got really good at roller skating. I loved it. Then we moved to a town in Arizona where there was no place to skate. There was a roller rink in Phoenix, but I was too shy to go because people would look at me. I went a couple of times, but I couldn't take it so I stopped. I didn't skate for about a year and was miserable. Finally I forced myself to and I'm so glad I did because now I'm in the Arizona Roller Derby Surly Gurlies. And you can't be shy there! Persistence paid off.

–Babs B., Chandler, Arizona

My telephone Round Two: I made some simple calls: the grocery store to ask their hours; the bus station to ask the schedule; the department store to ask if they carried slippers.

Telephone Round Three: By the end of the next week, I was ready to make a real call. My cherished little Siamese cat Louie had been acting sluggish. I phoned the vet and made an appointment.

Louie lived a long and happy life. That was my reward for conquering phone fear.

Thank you, God, you pulled through on your promise to "help those who help themselves."

"OH, I'LL JUST SKIP THIS ONE"

If you find a challenge exceptionally difficult, do not think, *I'll just skip this one and come back to it*. Every single ShyBuster in *Good-Bye to Shy* is designed to be doable. You don't need to follow the order in the book. But to be effective, you must do each ShyBuster in the order you assigned yourself. The first failure, the second, and even the third or more are all steps to your eventual success.

I'm sure you've heard the adage, "It's not whether you win or lose, it's how you play the game." The Baseball Commission might not agree, but the idea is accurate as you begin your battle. If you tackle a tough situation and fail, don't be discouraged. Take a deep breath and vow to succeed before the sun sets. If you don't, you must do it twice the next day.

ShyBuster #31
Don't Skip, Shirk, or Accept Defeat

If you find a challenge exceptionally difficult, do not skip it or chuck it. It can be habit forming and you'll be saying "Hello" to Shy again.

To gain confidence, you must do each ShyBuster pretty much in the order you assigned yourself. You designed your own program. Vow to stay with it! If you skip one step, go back and do it twice the next day.

It is not important you do it now. It is important that you envision and will someday do it.

—George Balanchine

PART

5

Four *Rare* ShyBusters That Work Wonders!

The following four extraordinary ShyBusters are based on a little-known but very powerful principle. They will let you interact with people in all sorts of different situations—and you'll have no fear that they are judging you. In fact, they don't even know who you are! You can try on different personalities like trying on shoes.

It is based on the potent and proven "anonymity effect."

> *Temporary anonymity is an excellent step*
> *for the extremely shy.*[26]
>
> –Philip G. Zimbardo

I've sat next to strangers on long bus rides who have told me their life stories, sometimes with scandalous secrets that they would never share with a friend. The only thing that they *didn't* tell me was their names. Take advantage of the courage that the anonymity effect gives everyone.

This first of these four extraordinary, no-pain Shy-Busters involves a real mask. In the next two, you'll wear a psychological mask. In the fourth ShyBuster, you shed the psychological mask and everyone recognizes you as the person you, perhaps even subconsciously, crave to be.

—— • ——

The Masked Shy

One of the sharpest pains of shyness is the fear of what people will think of you. But when nobody recognizes you as "you," it takes the sting out of interacting with other people. You can do or say whatever you want and not feel like people are judging you.

"WHO, ME? I'M 'MR. NOBODY.'"

Realizing this, one of the world's leading shyness experts had great success with a masking technique for his almost clinically shy little brother.[27] Little George Zimbardo was so shy that he would run and hide if anyone came to the house. He was miserable at school. He didn't make any eye contact, and he never played with the other kids.

His older brother Philip had an inspiration. He suggested that George might enjoy a special game, wearing a paper bag over his head with the eyes and mouth cut out. Little George loved the idea–so much so that he asked to wear the paper bag to school. The teacher agreed, saying that she would tell the other students it was for fun. When the other students asked George who he was, he would puff up his little chest and proudly answer, "Mr. Nobody."

The paper bag anonymity got George through the school year playing unself-consciously with the other kids. He was even able to be in the yearly circus production by wearing it.

Final proof of the power of anonymity: the following year, George performed one of the lead roles in the circus—without his face covered. By the time George was in high school, he had developed several close friendships. In his senior year, he was even elected to class office.

I'm not going to ask you to crawl around the mall wearing a mask, but do consider the proven remedial effect of temporary anonymity. When people don't know who you are, it's much easier to talk to them. And you get invaluable experience communicating with people you might normally be shy around. Like little George, you'll soon be ready to shed the "mask."

If the situation arises, attending a masked event, say a New Year's or Halloween party, is a good starting point.

MY NIGHT AS A RABBIT

It worked beautifully for me. One Halloween when I was teaching nursery school, the principal asked me to take some of the kids trick-or-treating. Just the thought of knocking on strangers' doors and making small talk with them while they dumped M&Ms into the kids' bags pushed my panic button. But I couldn't refuse.

I was in the Halloween department of a store buying decorations and plastic pumpkins for the class party. Staring back at the masks on the wall, inspiration hit. I could wear one while taking the kids trick-or-treating, and nobody would know that it was me!

It was wildly successful. Disguised as a rabbit, I was able to chat comfortably with people on their doorsteps as they dumped candy corn into the kids' bags. Once or twice, I even took the mask off when talking with a stranger. I felt vulnerable at those unmasked moments, and I still had difficulty making eye contact. But the bottom line was that the next year I was able to take the kids trick-or-treating without hiding behind a mask.

*Last summer I worked for a catering company and we all wore cos-
tumes, like old-fashioned butlers, cooks, and maids. Mine was a little
French maid outfit with a short skirt with ruffles and high heels. It surprised me so much that I didn't feel my usual shyness, even dressed like
that! I guess that was because when we were catering a party I didn't
know anybody—and in that getup, probably nobody would recognize me
anyway. It was so un-me.*

–Sandra V., Lexington, Mississippi

ShyBuster #32
Look for "Anonymous" Opportunities

If a masked ball or Halloween party comes up, don a costume that completely disguises you. Then approach other guests. Introduce yourself as
the character of your costume: "Hello, I'm Batman." "Hi, I'm the fairy
godmother!" "How do you do. I'm Godzilla." If you prefer a more "I'm a
live person under this ridiculous costume" approach, use a human-
sounding fake name. Anonymity is a priceless and proven way to practice
social skills and confident moves.

Naturally, the obvious opportunity to wear a mask comes but once a
year. So what can you do the other 364 days to benefit from the
anonymity effect?

(24)

How Can I Help You? . . . Help Me

You can step up from being "totally anonymous" to "almost anonymous." How? Arrange situations where you are interacting with people but they are not necessarily seeing you as "you."

Take a part-time job as a cashier, delivery person, valet car parker, or one of the dozens of other jobs that entail constant interaction. You can practice eye contact, smiles, and small talk with people. And the beauty of it is, they're not judging you. They're only concerned that you give them their correct change, bring their groceries on time, or don't bang up their car.

In high school and college, I worked as a cashier in a drugstore, a waitress in a greasy spoon, and a shampoo girl in a hair salon. Each job had increasingly longer interaction with the customers. I wasn't being judged on my personality or looks. I was being viewed as the anonymous cashier, waitress, or girl who shampooed hair.

As a shampoo girl, I got quite comfortable talking with some of the patrons. Maybe it was because the women weren't as intimidating when they smelled like permanent wave solution and had dozens of little pink rollers affixed to their heads. Whatever the reason, the shampoo experience was one more step in washing away my shyness.

If your schedule doesn't allow time for a part-time job, go for a weekend job. Restaurants and stores often hire extra help for their busy Friday evenings and Saturdays. Simple conversations build courage. "Do you want mustard and mayo with that burger?" "Would you like that gift-wrapped?" "Do you want our nine-dollar new-looking jeans or our hundred-dollar pretorn ones?"

I'm a pretty big guy, five-foot-eleven and 220 pounds. That makes it all the worse being shy. A buddy of mine owns a disco, and one night I got this call from him saying that his bouncer didn't show up and would I fill in. I did and I didn't feel shy at all that night. People thought of me as "the bouncer" that night, not as Freddie. I've filled in a couple of weekends since then and I think it's helped.

–Fred H., Baltimore, Maryland

ShyBuster #33
Take a Part-Time Job

Take an evening or weekend job working with people. Make it a situation where you are being judged not as "you" but as the role you are playing: department store salesperson, door-to-door survey taker, taxi driver. The "anything-but-totally-me" experience is a great way to get people practice in a safe, nonjudgmental environment.

If taking a part-time job isn't feasible for you, the next chapter has another no-painer to achieve similar results.

The Out-of-Town Caper

We could rename this section, "Excuse Me, I'm Anonymous in This Berg So I Can Make an Absolute Donkey of Myself and Nobody Will Give a Darn." But that's a tad long for a title.

"EXCUSE ME, I'M A STRANGER IN TOWN"

Look at situations from your jitters list (ShyBuster #16), which you have already categorized from the least intimidating to the most. Suppose that your inventory looks something like this:

- Asking strangers questions on the street
- Shopping and not buying something for fear I'll disappoint the salesperson
- Making eye contact and smiling at people I don't know
- Getting into extended small talk with a stranger
- Having an unpleasant or confrontational conversation

Tuck the list in your pocket or purse. Then hop in a car, bus, or train and travel to a nearby town where there's zip, nada, zero chance anybody knows you. Now, like a grocery list of things to buy, flip out your list and start doing everything on the page.

If the jitters list above were yours, you would assign yourself to:

- **Ask five people for directions.** Approach five passersby on the street and ask them for directions. If it helps your acting, carry a map and wear a confused expression to make it more convincing. That's good for an hour of communicating.
- **Try something on.** Try on three pairs of shoes at several shoe stores but don't buy any of them. Let's say that's another hour.
- **Smile at salespeople.** Go to a department store. Make eye contact with and smile at every salesperson and even some customers as you pass. Pretend to be shopping and ask about lots of different items in the store. You could spend two hours doing that.
- **Get product recommendations.** Ask a pharmacist which is the best cream for poison ivy. Do it at every drugstore in town. Another hour.
- **Ask about the lunch specials.** When you're having lunch, have the server describe the various dishes to you. That's a good five minutes if you stretch it out.
- **Talk to other passengers.** Take a bus ride and talk to the person sitting next to you. That's about ten minutes. Transfer to another bus and do the same. And another. And another.

Add another hour or two of scary stuff, and, if my math is right, you've had eight hours of constant communicating. After all of that interacting in another town, how much do you want to bet it's going to be a lot easier to talk to people in your own town the next day?

You may be thinking, "But what if someone asks my name?" Look at it this way. It is socially acceptable for a woman not to tell her age. It is generally expected that a fisherman will add an inch or two to the "big one" he caught. So you have dispensation to give a fake name if asked. It's therapeutic!

ShyBuster #34
Take a Trip to Anonymity-ville

Head straight for a town where nobody knows you. It's even better than wearing a mask because there is absolutely no risk of anyone recognizing you. Now practice all of the situations that usually put you in crisis mode. Talk to salespeople. Ask passersby for directions. Grill the waiter about the dinner special. When you return home, you'll be that much more comfortable talking to people in familiar territory.

Dress as Your Fantasy Person

Everybody goes to their closet in the morning and sleepily says to themselves, *Let's see, how do I feel today? What shall I wear?* You've heard the phrase "You are what you eat." Well, an even more visible verity is "You feel like what you're wearing."

The CEO of a major corporation wants to be respected, so he pulls out his dark suit. A woman, when she wants to feel sexy, snatches a hot dress to reveal her assets. And kids think they're cool wearing whatever the other kids who think they're cool are wearing.

YOU FEEL LIKE WHAT YOU WEAR

Just like everyone else, you go to your closet in the morning and mumble the same question, "How do I feel today?"

I ran a computer search for the words "I feel" through the e-mail I received from Shys. Sadly, I found "I feel dull," "I feel foolish," "I feel stupid," "I feel inferior," "I feel worthless," and "I feel like a side-show freak."

So, if you feel that way, then standing in front of your closet each morning you are *subconsciously* saying, *Let me find some clothes that make me look dull, foolish, stupid, inferior, worthless, or like a side-show freak.* Your hands instinctively go for dull duds–and naturally, people judge you by the way you dress.

WEAR "LOOK AT ME" CLOTHES

The solution? Recapture the spirit of fun kids have when they play dress-up. "I want to be a princess." "I want to be a pirate." "I want to be a policeman." And they tug the princess, pirate, and policeman costumes out of the trunk.

Do the same. Reaching for your daily duds, say to yourself, "I feel confident today." Grab garments like your favorite Sures wear. Better yet, dress with flair or fun. Wear something that makes people turn and look at you.

Anything goes these days. Men, you've always wanted to wear a cape like Jean Val Jean in *Les Misèrables*? Women, you admire perfect pedicures and those sexy, strappy, high-heel sandals? Go for it! If your budget is tight, you probably already have some accessories in your wardrobe that will give you flair. For example, women, tie a bright scarf elegantly at your neck. It says, "I feel good about myself."

When you get used to it, you'll be amazed at the confidence "look at me" clothing brings you.

Let's face it, a suit and a nice pair of shoes can work wonders in how we are going to feel in any social situation. I really think investing in a good wardrobe is going to boost someone's confidence. Why do you think James Bond is always wearing a suit?

–Dimitri D., Athens, Greece

Of course, it doesn't have to be a suit. But Dimitri is being faithful to his self-image, and that's what we all should aim for.

My husband and I have been married for eighteen years. Last July we went out to dinner, and as usual I was wearing a blouse that covered me up. They had outdoor tables and we were sitting at one. Underneath my blouse I was wearing a bra and slip and it got so hot I unbuttoned the top few buttons. My husband looked at my cleavage, and I thought his eyes were going to pop out. He said, "Honey, those are some boobs. Why do you keep them covered up all the time?" I don't know what got into me but it was the time when "slip tops" were popular. I slipped off my blouse and nobody noticed because it was the style. But my husband sure noticed it. When we got home that night, we made love for the first time with the lights on and I didn't feel self-conscious at all. He was so hot that it turned me on. Now I go around the house in just my slip and bra sometimes and I bought some sexier clothes. It really helped my self-image. I don't feel anywhere near as shy about my body as I used to. I even like going out dressing sexy.

−Donna I., Port Huron, Michigan

Go, Donna!

PART

6

For Big-Time Sufferers:
Get a (New) Life

Sorry to open this part with such distressing facts. But you want me to tell it like it is, right? I hope you know that I'm giving you the following information as a further incentive to say "good-bye to shy."

A report from the American Psychological Association revealed that even brilliant and talented Shys are at a great professional disadvantage. The report, entitled "Social Phobia and Difficulties in Occupational Adjustment," referenced dozens of studies by the world's foremost shyness researchers.[28]

The bottom line is that Shys are generally undervalued and underpaid for their talents. They are less apt to get a job that utilizes their education and abilities. And Shys' careers are more unstable right on through midlife.

That's chilling.

———— • ————

Just Something to Consider

REVELATION ON THE POTTY

When I was teaching nursery school, I loved walking confidently into the classroom and being greeted by a sea of happy little faces. Now I do realize that being confident around four- and five-year-olds is not an achievement of major magnitude, but I was very comfortable with my little munchkins.

There was, however, a problem—I began to talk like them. My only adult exposure was the third Monday of the month at PTA meetings. During one of our Parent-Teacher summits, I had to go to the restroom. As I stood up, I said, "Excuse me, I have to go to wee wee."

I could hear muffled tittering as I headed for the "potty."

That did it. Right there in the loo, I decided to quit teaching at the end of the semester and enter the "adult world." Mingling with the under-six set was doing nothing for my shyness, not to mention my vocabulary. I was in a contented rut. But I knew that I had to move on if I was going to be shy-free.

On my last day, we had a little party in the classroom. We all hugged and kissed and said "Bye bye, I wuv you" to each other. Then off I went into the scary adult world.

If you are miserable big-time over your shyness and your job isn't helping the situation, perhaps it's time to do something about it. Here are more distressing facts.

THE PROFESSIONAL WORLD CAN SHAFT SHYS

You probably undervalue yourself professionally and, according to the statistics, your employer does, too. Employers often gives Shys the short end of the stick.

If you're ready to look your work life squarely in the face, give yourself a professional interview. Ask yourself these serious questions:

1. Is my 9-to-5 life exacerbating my shyness?
2. Am I doing work beneath my capability?
3. Is my job utilizing my talents and education?
4. Am I having difficulty adjusting to my present job?
5. Could I get a job more in sync with my life goals?

And, of course the most relevant question of all . . .

6. Am I in a position to be able to switch jobs?

Most people are not able to consider a job switch at the moment. But do this ShyBuster anyway.

ShyBuster #36
Take a Second Look at Your Job

Answer the six questions listed above. Then, depending on the results, put on your thinking helmet to tackle some tough decisions. You may decide that you need a job change. Even if it's not the right time for that, your insights on your professional life can help you make healthier choices even within your current job. Your answers could plant seeds that grow relevant in the future. And, in the long run, this could turn out to be one of the most life-changing ShyBusters of all.

"NO JOB" STRESS

Don't jump ship, of course, unless you have a safe lifeboat to land in. Unfortunately, I didn't follow my own advice. I stepped off the school porch into the ranks of the unemployed with nothing in sight to keep me afloat. To top it off, job interviews terrified me. By the time the leaves turned that fall, I'd have to be working, or I'd be out on the streets—and too shy to beg!

I wangled a few job interviews. The interviewers asked me the same questions: "What are your strengths and weaknesses?" My unspoken answer was, *I love little kids but I'm unbearably shy around adults.*

"Where do you want to be in five years?" I couldn't tell them my true answer: *Not shy!*

"Tell me about a situation when you had to learn something complicated in a short time." Telling them *I had to put together a Mickey Mouse mobile in five minutes before my class began* wouldn't impress the interviewers.

I soon realized that reading Mother Goose stories and chasing twenty kids around a playground didn't prepare me for life in the fast track.

SNEAKY WAY TO GET A SUPER JOB

After half a dozen interviews, the stress from not hearing "You're hired" made me as jumpy as a grasshopper on a griddle. However, I discovered an interesting advantage to interviewing with many companies. Each interview became easier because all of the interviewers asked, almost verbatim, the same questions!

I suspect that all Human Resources professionals attend the same "How to Intimidate Applicants" seminar. First they warm you up with casual questions, maybe even offer you coffee. Then, just when you're feeling all cozy, they lean back, squint their eyes, and start slinging so-called "insightful" questions at you.

Shys, if you're job hunting, buy or borrow a book on what interviewers ask. Better yet, save your money. You'll find their hackneyed "trick questions" all over the Internet.

It's easy to get wise to their interview act. Rehearse some astute-sounding answers for the inevitable, "What are your strong points and weak points?" Then brush up on the left hooks the interviewer is bound to slug you with. My personal pet peeve was when he or she would smugly say, "So tell me about yourself," then tilt back in the chair while I went blank.

ShyBuster #37
Learn the "Left Field" Questions

Run an Internet search with words like *job* or *interview questions* and variations on that theme. You'll be deluged with solid advice. Prepare yourself, of course, for the usual warm-up queries: "Where did you work?" "How long?" "Why did you quit?" But be on the lookout for some of those questions that seem to come out of "left field." They're all the same: "Your best quality?" "Your worst?" "Why should we hire you?" Yada yada yada. Then practice your answers in the privacy of your own home. Remember, "Preparation is the prescription for panic."

GO FOR THE *LAST* COMPANY ON EARTH YOU'D WORK FOR

The actual questions, however, are only part of the interview experience. You've heard that the standard advice for job hunters is: "Practice with your friends or family."

Sure, but then go one step further as I inadvertently did. Shys, here's the plan–*cheat!*

OK, I exaggerate. It is not exactly cheating. It is simply a deliciously devious way to get the job you deserve. The gambit? First, interview with five or six companies you wouldn't dream of working for.

Your interview with the first company will be terrifying.

Your interview with the second company will be scary.

Your interview with the third company will be intimidating.

But by the fourth company, you'll be getting wise to them. You'll know their questions. You'll know their demeanor. And you'll know their game. After a few more dry runs with companies you don't want, you will be prepared for your dream job interrogation.

ShyBuster #38
Interview with Companies You *Don't* Want

To assure that you get the job you deserve, interview with half a dozen companies that they couldn't pay you enough to work for. When you feel like you know their game, go for the gold—interview for the job you really want.

During my corporate quest, I couldn't stop my thoughts from drifting back to my teenage fantasy of being a flight attendant. In those days, it was glamorous. Flight attendants didn't have to hawk headsets or keep the peanuts-per-passenger ratio as low as possible. Those were the days when "airline food" was not an oxymoron.

The more I thought about it, the more ideal it seemed. Shyness was my greatest challenge, and being a flight attendant was the answer. I'd have to deal with planeloads of grown-up passengers–saying "Hello! Welcome," then "Good-bye, thanks for flying with us" a hundred times in a row.

Pan American Airways was my dream. However, after the inspiration I had about interviewing with companies that I didn't want first, I booked interviews with American, United, TWA, and a few other dearly departed airlines. By the time I went to Pan Am, I had learned the airlines' most important qualification. In those days, it was a perpetual smile. I went in grinning like a chipmunk and got the job.

I found myself giving coffee, tea, and comfortable conversation to thousands of passengers.

ShyBuster #39
Consider a "People Profession"

In considering any job, visualize how much contact with the public you will have. The more contact, the more effective a shyness shedder it will be. You'll find off-the-job conversing a lot easier if you have to do lots of it on the job.

Then, of course, once you've shed all shyness, go for an interesting and enjoyable job that challenges you in other ways. Make sure that it utilizes your knowledge and talents.

PART

7

Parties and Other Places in Hell

The very mention of the "P" word can drive a stake into the hearts of Shys well on their way to recovery. Invite them to a party where they don't know anyone, and it mainlines queasiness into their veins. Smiling, being introduced to people, making small talk, flirting . . . arrrrrrgh!

Wait a minute. Come back. Do the following Shy-Busters, and, I promise, you'll soon look forward to parties and gatherings of all sorts.

———— • ————

Building Up to Big Bashes

In spite of the social strides I was making with passengers above the clouds, a party was still a living nightmare to me. As a flight attendant, I had a "role," things that I had to do, a reason for being there. However, everything that made me slump, sweat, and shiver all at the same time was embodied in one terrifying word–*parties*.

But, wouldn't you know it. As probably the shyest person who ever said "fasten your seat belt," I wound up living in a nonstop party building. It was near the airport and housed hundreds of us stewardesses. Legions of aspiring suitors nicknamed it "The Stew Pound."

Naturally, like any building housing a bevy of beauties, herds of hopeful men swarmed around it like bugs. Sadly, many ended up fried like insects in a bug zapper. But as much of a seller's market as it was, I was too shy to talk to even the grilled ones.

Annika and Ulla, two drop-dead gorgeous Scandinavians were my roommates. Every night they weren't on a trip, their ears would perk up at sounds of music, laughter, and clinking glasses somewhere in the building. With a splash of perfume and a dash of lipstick, they'd be prancing down the hall to find the party. I was rapidly running out of feeble excuses to stay home.

One evening, Annika was studying our flight schedules. "Oh, look at this. We're all going to be in town Thursday after next. Let's give a party!"

Drat, I knew this was going to happen sooner or later. "Wonderful idea!" I said.

The dreaded night arrived. About 6:30, Annika and Ulla excitedly helped each other with buttons, zippers, and makeup. I sat glued to my bed.

Annika looked at me, "Leil, aren't you getting dressed?"

"Uh, well, I have a good friend who has a bad cold," I lied. Mumbling something about bringing her chicken soup, I fled the apartment.

That night, sitting alone in a Chinese restaurant, I was miserable. I swore to attempt some of the parties in the building.

In the following weeks, I broke my self-promise dozens of times–until a lightbulb went on in my head. I devised a plan that miraculously shrank my fear of parties. Retroactively, I call it . . .

"PARTY LIKE A PIGEON"

Have you ever fed pigeons in the park? You cast a few bread crumbs on the path. Pigeons fly out of nowhere and apprehensively land about twelve feet away. In time, one brave bird bolts toward a crumb, grabs it in his beak, and flies away. The other pigeons see that their feathered friend survived the encounter. You cast another handful of crumbs. Some of the more courageous birds make tentative approaches. As their confidence grows, their distance from you diminishes. Before long, you're surrounded by peeping pigeons begging to eat out of your hand. Unbeknownst to them, of course, they've practiced "Graduated Exposure." They are no longer afraid of you.

Take a hint from the birds. Ease into a party. You can't just submerge yourself and expect not to drown. Don't flinch and say, "I will grin and bear it." That might be downright destructive because the pain could reinforce your fear of parties. It's too much, too soon. Instead, say, "I'll spend ten minutes there, that's all."

How painful can ten minutes be? You could survive ten minutes of the dentist drilling your teeth, right? But if he said, "Don't worry, I'm only going to keep drilling for three hours," you'd be sprinting down the street with the dentist's bib still around your neck.

At first, don't force yourself to stay at a gathering for an hour–then run like a frightened dog with its tail between its legs. Plan to spend only ten minutes at the first party. After you've done that, congratulate yourself and then leave. You can feel good about yourself because you've accomplished your goal.

Then, when the next gathering rolls around, increase your stay to twenty minutes, then thirty, and so on.

I'd like to have a relationship with a woman and I know parties are a major meeting place. But the idea of me striking up a relationship with a woman at a party is like science fiction because parties give me the jitters and I don't like to go to bars. A friend of mine invited me to go to a weekly mixer recently and I wasn't accustomed to mingling. I tried to stick with him but he was getting irritated that I was hanging on. I told him I was leaving. Then he dragged me there the next week and it wasn't as bad. . . . Now I'm trying to go each week and stay a little longer each time. I think it's helping because I don't shudder as much as the day approaches.

–Jeremy B., Abilene, Texas

"I HATE BIG PARTIES"

One reason that so many Shys shun parties is because the sheer number of people is overwhelming. They would feel more at ease with just a few. One Shy who wrote to me found a way to make even the biggest bashes less intimidating.

One thing that helped me get over being allergic to parties was to go early. That way I was forced to talk to people because there would be so few there.

–Ian E., Baltimore, Maryland

Great idea, Ian! An additional advantage to arriving early is that, as the party progresses, you now know a few people. If you start to get the jitters not knowing anyone, you can comfortably join them later. They can also introduce you to other partygoers. That's easier than making a "cold call" on a stranger standing nearby.

ShyBuster #41
Arrive Early While It's Still a Small Party

You don't like big parties? Most Shys don't at first. And they wouldn't dream of arriving early because they prefer to disappear in the crowd. Yet crowds are the big threat! Doesn't make sense.

Solution: arrive early when there are just a few people there. It's the perfect way to "make a big party small." You'll meet everyone there instead of having to approach people later. And you'll know people who can introduce you to others.

(29)

Don't Growl at the Guests

Whether it's a small gathering or a big bash, just plunking your body in the middle of it is not enough. If you're like many Shys, you may slump, look glum, and fold your arms in social situations. That position is not exactly a welcome mat. Then, when people don't approach you, you hate social gatherings all the more.

Women, think of it this way. If you spot a little kitten on the street, it takes a tough woman indeed to resist petting it. Then, if it doesn't look afraid, you might be tempted to pick it up and cuddle it. However, if kitty transmogrifies itself into a satanic Halloween cat with narrowed eyes and arched back, you might change your mind and walk away–fast.

Shys, you obviously don't hiss at the other guests. But not smiling and looking unapproachable works wonders to keep people away from you. Your demeanor shouts, "I'd rather be in Siberia."

Don't give yourself many brownie points for attending the party unless you keep your body language friendly and you take the initiative in conversations. Another problem with staying long enough at a party to become miserable is you might start speaking rapidly, standing stiffly, or clenching your fists to hide trembling.

Mental health professionals call nervous habits to try to hide shyness (such as averting your eyes, speaking rapidly, or clenching your hands to hide trembling) "safety behaviors." A study published in the *Journal of Behavioral Therapy*, "Maintaining Anxiety and Negative

Beliefs," tells us that the more we succumb to these defenses, the more they will increase shyness.[29]

Some Shys think that showing up at a party is enough. But just parking your bod in the middle of the bash is not "going to a party." If you look as tense as a turkey before Thanksgiving, it's no help.

ShyBuster #42
Set Yourself Specific Party Goals

When you go to a party, set yourself some goals, such as "look everyone in the eyes," "have a pleasant, relaxed expression on my face," "smile *broadly* at a few people—the host, an acquaintance, an attractive other." Set goals commensurate with the time you're staying, as per ShyBuster #40. You must introduce yourself to one person in the ten-minuter, two in the thirty-minuter . . . and so on. Ten minutes at the party practicing your social skills is far more effective than staying an hour and letting yourself get tense.

Personality Is Catching

CHAMELEONS SHOULD CHOOSE THEIR COLORS CAREFULLY

It is fiction that those cute microdinosaurs called chameleons change to match their surroundings. But it is fact that people change to match theirs. If you have a confident friend who has an out-going personality, you will become more gregarious, too—just by being around him or her. If your good buddy talks to strangers, you will start yapping it up with new people, too. If your cool friend goes to parties, you will find yourself tagging along. It's a simple case of monkey see, monkey do. (No insult intended!)

My friend Daffy was an extraordinary extrovert. And I was a shy but grateful little monkey trying to be as outgoing as she was. I know she played an important role in dissipating my shyness. If you don't cur-rently have an extroverted same-sex friend, make it a goal to find one.

There is very outgoing girl, Rachael, who works in the same office. We became friends and one night she dragged me out to a club that had dancing until 2 A.M. I wanted to leave but she was my ride home. Fortunately it was dark in the corners so I hid out there and watched everybody else dancing in the center of the room.

Rachael was actually walking up to guys and talking to them, and then they would dance. I always wanted to be like her but I was too shy.

She found me sitting in the corner and scolded me. I explained to her for the umpteenth time that I was shy. I don't know whether she was drunk or what but she seriously told me that she wasn't going to give me a ride home unless I went up to some guy and asked him to dance. I couldn't do that but I did manage to go talk to one. After that, I felt a little better and talked to several more. They seemed happy that I came over to them.

–Danielle B., Greenwich, Connecticut

I'd say that the next time Danielle goes to a club with Rachel, she won't hide in a dark corner. Taking your cues from a supportive and confident friend gives a big boost to your Stamping Out Shyness campaign. If Rachael had been shy, too, both women would have huddled together in the corner all evening being miserable.

ShyBuster #43
Find a Sociable Same-Sex Friend

It may not be conscious copy-catting, but, like chameleons are reputed to do, we do take on the colorations of those we hang with. It may be difficult, but it is definitely worth the time to find an extroverted same-sex friend. Then tell him or her that you welcome a little shove in new situations. But, when you are at the party, do NOT hang with them all evening. Make it a point to meet new people.

USE THE "BUDDY SYSTEM"

Naturally, unless you are a highly trained secret agent, it is difficult to hide insecurity. Professional body language court witnesses speak of "emotional leakage," emotions that slip out even though you think you are hiding them.

Do you remember the letter in Chapter 20 from Stephen, who thought he was smiling when he was at the club in California? He was astonished when a woman told him he looked dour. Another letter writer, Dina from Chicago, suffers a similar syndrome and came up with an interesting technique. She had a friend "monitor" her whenever she was slumping.

I am very tall for a girl, six-foot-one, and, since I am shy, I hate my height. I got into the habit of slumping and, although I would force myself to go to parties, no one ever asked me out. One time a girlfriend of mine told me not to hunch over so much. I caught a reflection of myself in the window and she was right. I felt much better and less shy when I stood up straight. From then on, I have asked her to help me with my posture and poke me every time she sees me slumping. P.S. I think she enjoys it!

—Dina F., Chicago, Illinois

You, too, can enlist the help of a friend. Ask him or her to give you an occasional visual checkup, not just on slumping, but on all of your nervous habits. If your friend notices you looking unfriendly or avoiding eye contact, ask to be told—or scolded!

Even better, set up a rewards program. Like airline miles, grant your friend a certain number of points each time he or she catches you. Enough points, you buy dinner or let your buddy decide on the reward. It's a great incentive for encouraging your friend to give you an even greater prize, the look of confidence.

ShyBuster #44
Have a Buddy Monitor Your Body Language

Could your smile be mistaken as a smirk? Is your eye contact quicker than a lizard's tongue? And what about your body language? Does it look like a "Private Property" or "Keep Out" sign?

Ask a chum to check you out periodically to keep you looking sociable and confident. Give him or her a checklist: folded arms, unfriendly expression, bad posture, avoiding looking at people, not smiling, and so on—whatever your particular nervous habits or safety behaviors might be. You might even offer a little incentive, monetary or otherwise, to make sure your friend stays on your case.

(31)

Shys and Booze Don't Mix

When we are in physical pain, we take medicine. Some Shys who suffer severe anguish turn to psychiatrists for medication. Since we are do-it-yourselfers, we are busting shyness through proven techniques without medication. Unfortunately, for some Shys, "doing it yourself" means medicating themselves–with beer, booze, or drugs. Here is a depressing statistic.

> Individuals with SAD (Social Anxiety Disorder) are at two to three times greater risk for alcohol abuse and dependence on other substance abuse disorders. They frequently use alcohol to self-medicate in order to decrease anticipatory anxiety and reduce avoidance of feared social and/or performance situations.[30]
>
> *–JOURNAL OF PSYCHIATRIC RESEARCH*

Drugs and alcohol can make a Shy feel more confident–but only for a very short time. You may think that people like you because they smile and clap while you're doing the hula on the coffee table. Men, you may think they're laughing because your jokes are so funny. But they're really laughing at you.

Women, you may feel like a femme fatale because men are flocking around you. But it's fatal to your ego when, the next day, you realize why. You can get a reputation of being "easy" or a lush.

I encountered a sad example of precisely that a few years ago when I was visiting a friend in my old hometown. While relaxing on Reenie's porch, a strikingly beautiful redhead came out of the door across the street.

Reenie looked over at her. "Meow. That's my new neighbor, Samantha—what a snob! If I say hi to her, she just looks the other way.

"Not that I lean out the window spying or anything, but I notice she has one boyfriend for a couple of weeks. Then he disappears and he's replaced by another, then another, then another. I guess she's real choosy."

"With those looks, she can afford to be."

"I suppose," Reenie grumbled. "But she could be a little nicer to us earthlings."

"I have an idea," I said. "Why don't we invite her to come join us on Saturday for a barbecue? We were planning to celebrate the Fourth of July in your backyard anyway. After all, she is your neighbor. And, hey, she might even introduce us to some of her rejects."

We left a note in Samantha's mailbox, never expecting to see her.

At noon on Saturday, we started the grill and put beer in the ice bucket. Behind us, we heard, "Yoohoo, it's me. Sammi."

Reenie and I whirled around, surprised to see her. Samantha continued in a slightly slurred voice, "Oh my goodness, those hot dogs smell dee-licious. They go so good with beer. May I have one?" She meant the beer, not the dogs. Not waiting for an answer, she headed straight for the cooler.

Reenie leaned over and whispered, "I think she's looped, and it isn't even noon yet!"

Several hours and several beers later—two beers each for us and six for Sammi—we started talking about, what else, men.

Reenie crooned the common lyrics, "Where are all the good men?" Drying mock tears, I joked, "I think they're all dating Sammi."

Sammi shocked us both when she announced, "Yes, but they always break up with me."

"Huh?" Reenie and I gulped in unison.

She looked down. "I'll meet a guy, usually at a bar. We'll go out a few times, but it always winds up the same. They accuse me of being an alcoholic and don't call me any anymore."

"Well," Reenie ventured tentatively, "do you, uh, drink a lot?"

"Well, I'm no fun without a few drinks. My dates would see me like I really am–boring and shy. I don't even talk to people at work."

Reenie and I looked at each other.

Sammi continued. "Ever since I was a kid, I've been a loner. It wasn't because I wanted to, but I couldn't look anyone in the eyes. In high school, I didn't have any dates until I started loosening up with a few drinks. Then I'd have a great time. When I started feeling uncomfortable, I'd just have another drink."

Our hearts went out to Sammi.

CONFIDENCE DISSOLVES IN ALCOHOL

Using alcohol to feel confident doesn't work in the long run. In fact, it makes the situation worse. Not only do you run the risk of becoming dependent on your "libation medication" or drugs, but you also deprive yourself of the satisfaction of having negotiated a social situation on your own. You feel all the more insecure the next time. Drinking can sink your confidence to a new low. Not to mention giving yourself a bad reputation and miserable hangovers.

ShyBuster #45
Drink "One Too Few"

Everyone's body has a different "Oops, one too many" level. If it's three beers, don't drink more than two. If it's two glasses of wine, don't go above one. If your "one too many" level is one, have a Coke or sparkling water. It's a sign of confidence. People respect you that you don't need a liquid "crutch."

Reenie has told me that Sammi looks much older than when I'd met her just a couple of years ago. Samantha is no longer a gorgeous redhead. Her dates have been dwindling off, and she seldom leaves the house except to go to work.

Here is another sad statistic: The *Journal of Anxiety Disorders* published a study showing super-shy people who drank to relieve the anguish of their shyness were far less likely to get married than the more sober Shys.[31] Sadly, that seemed like it was going to be Sammi's fate.

Fearless Conversation

It seems that the more brilliant and educated people are, the more they detest small talk. It's understandable. With so many deeper things to discuss, why waste brilliant breath with comments about the weather or asking others, "How are you?" (You know they really don't care.)

What you may not realize is that small talk has a vital role in communicating. It serves as an overture to more meaningful dialogue. It establishes a sense of "togetherness." Think of small talk like music, cats purring, children humming, or groups chanting. It gives you time to get a sense of the people you're talking to–their mood, their personality. It gives you clues in what direction to take the conversation.

But here's what most people forget. In all good music, it is the *melody*, not the lyrics that count.

— • —

Terrified to Be Trite?

BE A "ME-FIRSTIE"

Suppose that you see someone you know approaching. Your mind races. *Will I say something foolish? She'll think I'm stupid or boring. What if she says something to me and my mind goes blank? I'd better pretend I don't see her.*

Here's a novel idea. Why not just say, "Hi! How are you?" It's banal, of course, but it is the accepted form of greeting in our culture. Naturally, your acquaintance doesn't expect a real answer. She doesn't want to hear about your hernia or hemorrhoids. She just wants a simple, "I'm fine."

When it comes to acquaintances meeting on the street, the one who speaks first is definitely a winner. It makes the person you spoke to feel liked and respected. It makes you look confident. It subconsciously shows them that you have no fear of the encounter or any ensuing conversation. Whether this is true or not, speaking first radiates an attractive positive energy.

"UH, I'M FINE. HOW ARE YOU?"

When someone asks, "Hi, how are you?" you needn't give the parrot-like, "Fine, thanks. How are you?" (He'll say "Fine," and then both of you are standing there, looking at each other, and stuck for something to say.)

Don't fear that it is rude for you not to request that vital piece of information of how he or she is. Instead, respond quickly with the almost mandatory "fine," but then, hardly catching a breath, extend the interaction by commenting on something about your day. For example:

He: "Hi, how are you?"

You: "Fine. I'm really looking forward to the game tonight." (You've followed "fine" with an immediate comment.)

Then volley the conversational ball over the net with a question such as "Are you going to watch it?" Now you've asked a question, and the other person must respond. I call this the "Comment-Question" formula.

Believe it or not, even talking about the weather is OK. Eavesdrop on anyone, and you'll find that that is precisely what most conversation openings are all over the world.

She: "Hi, how are you?"

You: "Fine. I hear it's going to be warm and sunny this weekend." That's your *comment*. Then continue, "Do you have any special plans?" That's your *question*.

Even after such an inauspicious opening as the weather, something lovely happens. The more small talk two people make, the more apt it is to evolve into a more interesting discussion. Small talk is the precursor of bigger talk.

ShyBuster #47
Use the Comment-Question Technique

When someone asks, "How are you?" don't just respond with the traditional, "'I'm fine. And you?" That aborts the conversation before it ever takes off. Extend it by adding a sentence about your day. Then ask a related question and you immediately earn a place on his or her "confident and friendly colleagues" list.

(Note: if someone just gives you a "yes" or "no" answer to your question, continue with some "Keep Talking" questions, which we will explore in ShyBuster #51.)

What If I Have Nothing to Say?

You may be thinking, *What if the news of my day is mundane? Nothing interesting happened . . . is happening . . . or will happen.* Don't fret about that. Just deliver any humdrum news in an upbeat, I'm-thrilled-to-tell-you voice. After the predictable "How are you," you could declare with energetic mock exasperation, "Fine, but I've been traipsing all over town looking for a new briefcase, and I hate to shop." (Comment.) "Don't you?" (Question.)

Perhaps his response is that his brother-in-law just gave him a brief-case for his birthday. It's a snore, of course. But smile and respond like it's electrifying news. Ask him where his brother-in-law lives. Pretend that you're fascinated that he's from Podunkie. Ask what Podunkie is like. (Before you realize it, you're playing a good hand of small talk, the game that many Shys fear most.)

ShyBuster #48
Sound Dazzled over the Dullest Things

No matter how boring you think your statement is, present it in a this-is-the-greatest-thing-since-Velcro tone. And guess what? It will sound interesting to your listener. Conversely, no matter how boring *your acquaintance's* words are, respond like that's the most enthralling revelation you've heard all week. Now *you* will sound interesting to your listener.

Your Enthralling Answer to a Cliché Query

It's a sure bet. Within five minutes of meeting someone, she'll ask, "What do you do?" Don't flounder for the right words every time. Rehearse a concise, upbeat job description to make it sound like you do the most exhilarating work in the world.

Sadly, many Shys, when asked the inevitable, drop their eyes and say, "Oh, I'm just a . . ." Once I was visiting a company and got lost in the hall. A passing woman led me to my destination. I thanked her and said, "By the way, what department are you in?"

"I'm just the receptionist," she answered.

I wanted to shake her for seeing her job as unimportant. "No, you are not *just* the receptionist," I gently chided her. "You are *the* receptionist." She looked at me as though I were a little strange.

When someone asks the standard question "What do you do?" smile and sound passionate about your work. If someone is the CEO of a highly respected international firm and hates his or her work, that person will come off as a loser. On the other hand, if you love your work, even if you breed slugs for a living, you will sound like a winner. A winner in life is someone who is leading the life he or she loves. And all the world loves a winner.

ShyBuster #49
Rehearse Your Proud Minirésumé

Don't answer the inevitable "What do you do?" with just the name of your job. Plan a *proud* response and rehearse your upbeat minimonologue in the mirror. Then deliver it enthusiastically, as though it thrills you that someone asked you this novel question.

(35)

Voice Quality Counts, Too

What quality reveals shyness most? You probably answered "eye contact," and you are right. However, many Shys aren't aware that their voices run a photo-finish second. The volume, speed, and timbre of your voice are measures of your assurance—or lack of it. Confident people have more variety and resonance in their voices. Confident people have fewer uncomfortable pauses.

How you say something deafens people to *what* you say. When you speak in a hesitant voice, all they hear is, "What I'm saying is not very important."

When you pause midsentence, they hear, "I don't have my thoughts together."

When you hesitate, they hear, "I can't keep my mind on what you're saying because I'm too distracted by wondering what you think of me."

When you speak too fast, they hear, "I'd better race through this sentence before I get distracted thinking about myself again."

TELL YOUR GOLDFISH WHAT YOU HAD FOR BREAKFAST

Here's where your goldfish comes in handy again. Don't let the fact that it doesn't have ears dissuade you. You are merely rehearsing a smooth voice. Think of it like practicing a musical instrument. Every time you rehearse, the sound becomes stronger and smoother.

ShyBuster #50
Practice Storytelling on Your Goldfish

It doesn't have to be what you had for breakfast, of course. It can be anything.

Talk to your goldfish (or dog, cat, marsupial, or mirror) for five or six minutes in a voice with lots of energy and variety—and very few pauses. In conversations with humans, of course, you must have pauses so they can interject their thoughts. However, since your goldfish probably won't have anything interesting to interject, keep on talkin'.

So, What Do I Say Next?

BETTER THAN HUMANOID SOUNDS

With the following ShyBuster, you will never anguish again about what to say next. Most people, while *supposedly* listening to someone talk, make various humanoid sounds: "Hmm," "Uh huh," "OK," "Oh yeah?" "You don't say!" Unfortunately, Shys have a difficult time making these comforting noises because they're concerned about what the speaker might think of them. Here's a technique that everyone, not only Shys, could benefit from. For Shys, it's a foolproof remedy to keep a stalling conversation running smoothly.

Instead of being a run-of-the-mill hummer, have some "keep talking" questions ready. I call them the WWWWW and H queries: "Who?" "What?" "When?" "Where?" "Why?" and "How?" questions work wonders to keep others talking when a pause occurs. You might ask:

"*Who* gave you that?"

"*What* did she say then?"

"*When* did you realize that?"

"*Where* did you find it?"

"*Why* did you choose that school?"

"*How* did you accomplish that?"

It's a win-win situation. Most people love to hear their favorite music–their own voices. They will keep talking longer. And you won't suffer the excruciating "What do I say next?" syndrome.

Here's the ever-reliable WWWWW and H formula in action. Mr. Snore is bragging about his vacation to Italy. You ask:

"Who were you traveling with?"

"What was your favorite city?"

"When did you go—what season?"

"Where did you go in Italy?"

"Why did you choose Italy?"

Recently I was gabbing away at someone and realized that the poor guy hadn't said a word. I paused to give him a chance. He just said, "Go on, Leil. Tell me more."

Wow! I didn't need a second invitation. I delved into another twenty-minute monologue and came away thinking that *he* was an intriguing conversationalist.

I used to be afraid of small talk and always felt people wanted to get away from me because I was so quiet. One thing that helped me get over my fear of making small talk with strangers is realizing that they really weren't concerned with my opinion. What do they care? I learned they loved it when I asked them an occasional question about what they were saying.

—Ralph G., Greenville, Kentucky

ShyBuster #51
Ask "Keep Talking" Questions

Leave "uh huh" and "OK" to the robot crowd. Throw out some "Who?" "What?" "When?" "Where?" "Why?" and "How?" questions. Your conversational companion will be thrilled that you want to hear more—and you won't feel pressured to come up with convivial and clever conversation.

BANAL IS GOOD; BRIEF IS NOT

While you're at it, prime yourself for the inevitable banal interrogation. Do not give one-word answers like these . . .

"Where are you going for vacation this year?" *Florida.*

"How's your Mom (Dad, kid, brother, sister, spouse, parakeet)?" *Fine.*

Such stunted answers are guaranteed ways to snuff out conversation. Plan longer answers like, "Well, we were thinking of going to the Caribbean, but we decided that was too expensive. Then we saw this brochure on Florida. But there were so many possibilities in Florida. So we . . ." And off you go.

ShyBuster #52
Be Banal but *Not* Brief

Don't get bogged down worrying about the content of your answers to commonplace questions. Plan answers ahead of time to questions you know you'll be asked, then be prepared to answer with a paragraph, not a word.

Are people really fascinated by the intricate workings of your mind and how you came to the momentous decision to visit Disney World? Probably not. But, as you remember, it's the music that counts, not the lyrics. A long answer is a friendly tune.

Using *Their* Name Says a Lot About You

In spite of the millions of times people have heard their own name, hearing it roll off your tongue makes them feel warm and fuzzy. But did you know that it also says a lot about you? Subliminally they hear, "I am confident. I like you. I respect you. And we are friends."

Understandably, as with mastering any new skill, it's difficult to gauge how many times to say the other person's name in conversation. Soon you'll get the feel of when it's appropriate. For now, lay it on them at the greeting and the parting. "Good morning, Name." "Good to see you, Name." "So long, Name." "Nice talking with you, Name."

Be careful, however. If you utter their names too much, you could come across as insincere and condescending. Not to mention annoying.

I had a problem with my computer several months ago. I called tech support to report that every time I tried to open a file, I'd get an error message. The conversation went something like this:

Techie: OK. What's your name?

Me: Leil.

Techie: Are you sitting in front of your computer now, Leil?

Me: Yes, I am.

Techie: Good, Leil. Now double click on "My Computer."

Me: OK, I've done that.

Techie: Leil, now I want you to click on "Folders." Have you done that, Leil?

Me: Yes.

Techie: Now, Leil, scroll down to the directory the file is in.

Me: OK. (While wanting to shout, "Alright, already, I know what my %#&$ name is!")

Techie: OK. Now I want you to double click on the file that you can't open, Leil.

At this point, I wanted to double click on his head with a hammer.

With a little practice, you'll quickly get a sense of when to use someone's name and when not to. As your confidence grows, so will your sensitivity to subtleties like this. For now, twice is fine.

ShyBuster #53
Use Their Moniker—in Moderation

Say someone's name in greeting and parting. It makes him or her feel as warm and fuzzy as a furball. But beware—if you use it too much, it comes across as a nervous habit and makes that someone feel as warm and fuzzy as a Brillo pad.

It's All Sooo Predictable

MY "D'UH" MOMENT

Coming back from a party recently, I had a blinding flash of the obvious. After all of these years, like in the comic books, a light-bulb appeared above my head. Practically *all* of the conversations at parties are about the same old stuff: Movies. Marriages. Kids. Pets. Vacations. Sports. Celebrities. The most recent national disaster.

Sometime partygoers venture into more learned subjects, such as the thirteen tombs of the Ming Dynasty or the big bang theory of the universe. But most conversation is mundane and very, very predictable. That's super news for Shys. Pondering my dazzling discovery, ShyBuster #54 was born.

Make a mental list of all of the possible subjects that could come up at a party. Check the Internet to become informed on each. If the subject relates to current events, scan the headlines from your favorite media. A television newscast? Radio? Newspaper? Don't wait until the conversation to frame your thoughts on the latest political scandal or celebrity divorce. Formulate your philosophy on these earth-shattering events ahead of time. If you wait to do it on the spot, the gang will be dishing some other dirt by the time you open your mouth.

ShyBuster #54
Contemplate Before the Conversation

It's not enough to know "They're rioting in Africa, they're starving in Spain, there are hurricanes in Florida, and Texas needs rain." Make a complete list of possible conversational subjects. You needn't ponder erudite answers or plan polemic worthy of the Harvard debating team. However, develop a clear conviction about each subject on your list. Formulate and update it every day so that you can dive into the discussion like a Sure, without awaiting a formal invitation.

Your Turn for the Kick-Off

GO AHEAD, GET OPINIONATED

Now we graduate to bringing up a subject in conversation, not just discussing what other people introduce.

You've heard people complaining that someone is "too opinionated." Most likely that's not your problem. Most Shys are not opinionated enough. That very fact gives you an unrestricted license to start forming strong opinions on matters.

Start by listing your principles and interests. Perhaps it is your conviction that global warming is just a myth or that computer games are educating our kids. On the other hand, you might feverently feel that global warming will fry the planet or that computer games will lead to future generations being legless.

Then think each opinion through and the reasons you feel that way. Surf the Internet for some substantiating arguments. Articulate these elements to yourself. Then figure out ways you can casually turn the conversation to those topics you are knowledgeable about.

YOU'RE NOT DONE YET

A quick recap. You are now:

- Saying "Hi" or "How are you?"to people first (ShyBuster #46);
- Interjecting an immediate comment after you say, "I'm fine" or whatever (ShyBuster #47);
- Following it up with a question to get the other person talking (ShyBuster #47);
- Having an energetic, up-beat voice when you talk—and sounding absolutely dazzled by what others say (ShyBuster #48);
- Giving an enthusiastic "I just love my job" answer to the inevitable question, "And what do you do?" (ShyBuster #49);
- Asking some of the WWWWW and H queries ("Who?" "What?" "When?" "Where?" "Why?" and "How?") to keep your conversational partner going (ShyBuster #51);
- Saying the other person's name at the beginning and end of the conversation (ShyBuster #53);
- Contemplating what you'll say when all the common topics come up (ShyBuster #54);

- Never giving brief answers to banal questions, but stretching your answers out (ShyBuster #52);
- And, finally, planning how to bring up some topics that excite you (ShyBuster #55).

But there is one more element to being a confident and charismatic conversationalist.

The Final Conversational "Gotta Do"

Now here is the must. After you've stated your opinion, ask your conversational partners what they think. Many Sures neglect to do this and, as a result, can be considered bores who don't listen to anyone else's view.

Researchers for a study called "The Behavioral Assessment of Social Competence in Males" chose two groups of men.[32] The first group was made up of well-liked men who dated a lot. The second group consisted of subjects who were not popular.

The researchers directed all of the men to have conversations with women at a dance and then to ask them for a date. The guys' chats were recorded with hidden microphones.

Generally, when the more popular men finished offering their opinion on a certain topic, they asked the woman how she felt about the subject. The more unpopular men did not. Incidentally, an overwhelming number of women said "yes" when the men in the first group asked them for a date. Few of the men from the second group got a "yes."

Obviously this advice doesn't just go for opposite-sex dialogue. To be respected and liked, you should do this with everyone.

ShyBuster #56
Bat the Ball Back to Your Listener

After using all of the ShyBusters to become an excellent conversationalist, don't forget one of the most important elements. Be sure to turn the conversation around and ask your listener how he or she feels about a particular topic. Listen to his or her opinion. Then follow up with some thoughts on what he or she has said. Then repeat this ShyBuster over again. That's what comfortable and confident communicating is all about!

If you keep practicing the Fearless Conversation ShyBusters, one night as you are dozing off, you'll sit bolt upright. "Amazing–I didn't even think about my conversations today! They all came so naturally." That is the jubilant night you can fall asleep realizing that you will soon be shy-free.

(41)

Some of the Best Conversationalists Never Open Their Mouths!

I want to share an encouraging truth with you. As you practice the various conversation techniques, of course, you will find each exchange more comfortable. But until you're feeling pretty positive about your cool communicating, keep in mind that you don't always have to talk to make a good impression.

Just a few months after my friend Daffy's life-changing eye contact training, we were talking on the phone about it. "Daf, I cannot tell you how easy it is now to look at all my passengers. Bingo—right in the eyes!"

As I was blithering on, Daffy got that familiar "I've-got-something-up-my-sleeve" sound in her voice.

"Can you come over in about an hour?" she asked.

"Well, sure, but . . ." She'd already hung up.

When I arrived, Daffy notified me, "Today you're taking your next step toward your doctorate in confidence." I could tell that she was enjoying playing her new role as my therapist.

"My mother is giving a small luncheon party today and . . ." Terror must have filled my face, because she continued, "Don't worry, Leil, it won't be so bad. This time, in addition to eye contact, I want you to listen carefully to whoever is speaking. Then you will smile and nod when appropriate."

"But I can't make small talk with strangers, just like that."

"Here's the beauty of it, Leil. You won't have to. My mom volunteers for an organization that orients new immigrants. Today is a welcome lunch for fourteen of them, and I don't think even one speaks English. So, don't you see? The pressure is off. You don't have to say a word. Just smile, act friendly, and look them in the eyes."

We arrived at a bustling Greek tavern, and it seemed that everyone was talking simultaneously in a language that was, well, Greek to me. Daphnis's mother was sitting at a large table with the new arrivals. Daffy gave her a kiss on the cheek and introduced me. Her mother suggested that I sit near her because I didn't speak any Greek.

YOU ARE NOT EXPECTED TO PERFORM

Daffy winked. "Absolutely not. I'm putting Leil right over there between Leonidas and Scopas." I felt as though I was being abandoned in a cage with lions.

When we were introduced, they smiled broadly. I smiled weakly.

"Don't worry," Daffy whispered to me, "I told them you didn't speak Greek. I'm going over to sit with Mom now."

"Daf, don't leave me!" But she was gone.

The waiter put a strange dish in front of me that looked like octopus with some kind of cold sauce. In sign language, Leonidas asked me if I liked it. I managed to swallow the slimy thing while nodding my head dramatically. I even clapped my hands softly to show that I loved it.

I couldn't believe how relaxed I was getting. My self-appointed, nonaccredited therapist would be proud of me. For the first time while sitting at a table with a group of people, I didn't want to be invisible. In fact, I sat up tall, pushed my hair back, and even smiled at one of the good-looking Greek guys at the other end of table.

Then it got hairy. The hot Greek excused himself from his dinner partners and headed straight toward me. I panicked. *What if he speaks English? What if I have to talk to him?*

He bowed graciously and introduced himself in Greek. Daffy raced to the rescue. He spoke briefly to her, and Daffy beamed at me. "Leil, Tylissus wants to ask you for a date."

"Who wants to do what?"

"He's serious."

"You've got to be kidding, Daf! Tell him that's very nice of him. I'm flattered. But, Daf, tell him I'm married. Tell him I have a communicable disease. Tell him *anything*!"

Daffy somehow extricated me. As the party grew to a close, everyone took my hand, smiled at me, and said "good-bye" in Greek. Because I was a warm, receptive listener, the fact that no sounds came out of my mouth was hardly noticeable. Most of them didn't even know that I didn't speak a word of Greek.

On the way back to Daffy's place, I announced that I didn't feel at all uneasy at the party.

"Of course not!" she said. "Nobody expected you to say anything."

That whacked me like a killer wave. She was right! I didn't have to *perform*. No one expected me to speak. And no one was going to judge me by what I said.

NO ONE WILL NOTICE YOU DIDN'T SPEAK

Shys, you would have the same experience if your luncheon companions didn't speak English. You wouldn't fear that you'd say something stupid or inappropriate. If they were strangers and you knew you wouldn't see them again, you'd feel more relaxed.

Well, guess what? Even when everyone in a group is speaking crystal-clear English, and some of them know you, you are not expected to perform. You don't have to say anything if you don't want to. But you must listen, smile, and nod. That flags your friendliness. The more nods and smiles you bestow on them, the better personality they'll know you have.

I have a good friend, Nate. Nate doesn't talk much. But whenever I tell him *anything*, he gives me an enormous grin and says "Really?" or "That's great"—as though my lame comment really were. It is such a pleasure being around Nate. A beautiful and brilliant attorney, Deborah, apparently thinks so, too. They just got married.

I once asked Deborah how they'd met. She told me Nate was one of her clients. "I'd never met such a good listener. He's so much fun," she said. "And he has that big goofy smile." I knew she meant "lovable."

How to Forget Being Shy

PASSION SLAYS SHYNESS

When you are totally passionate about something, you don't even notice when you are talking. All you know is that you need to get your ideas across. When you are speaking about something you are enthusiastic about, your shyness takes a back seat. In fact, it flies right out the back window and evaporates into thin air.

I discovered this remedial effect passion has on shyness when I was twelve years old. Two boys, Donny and Bobby Baker, lived next door. They teased me mercilessly and constantly. Whenever they played outside, I raced into the house.

Doing my homework on the porch one Saturday afternoon, I heard boisterous laughter in their backyard. As usual, I scooped up my books to hide out inside. Just then, I heard an animal's piercing scream. I spun around.

There was Bobby, gleefully swinging a screeching stray cat by the tail while his little brother sprayed it with a garden hose. Not for a split second did shyness enter my consciousness. I dropped my books and my papers scattered across the porch as I shrieked at them like a hawk out for blood.

They laughed and held the tortured creature up for me to get a better view. That did it. Full of fury, I snatched a shovel by the garage door, raised it over my head, and took off after them.

Flabbergasted, they dropped the cat and ran. The poor creature scurried away, hopefully back to its family to be licked back to health.

It wasn't until I returned to my porch that I felt the menacing weapon in my hands. I stared at it in disbelief. My passion for animals had momentarily overcome my shyness.

Years ago, I started DJ'ing parties at my fraternity house. I was so involved in the music that it was easy to talk to women that I used to be afraid to talk to. They even came up to me for requests. That helped me to feel more comfortable about myself.

–Buddy C., Los Angeles, California

"I DIDN'T THINK ABOUT MYSELF ALL EVENING"

Books often suggest that going to seminars is a good antishyness strategy. They recommend offering to hand out programs, take tickets, and so on. It's good advice. In fact it's very good advice. If your main purpose for being there, however, is to practice mingling, you're still watching "The Me Show." Thinking back, if I had been at a People for Persecuted Animals meeting instead of simply sitting on my back porch, I would probably have been fixated on myself, not victimized animals, when Bobby and Donny showed up.

The point is that when you are totally passionate about something, you forget yourself because you're so absorbed in your purpose.

I am forty-eight and, when I was divorced eleven years ago, I found it impossible to get back into the dating scene. I was too shy to go to parties or even think of approaching a man. I have always loved wine and consider myself something of a connoisseur. Just recently I've started going to wine tastings and have met several very nice men. It's so easy to talk to them because they love wine, too, and we have something to talk about.

–Donna F., Martinsburg, West Virginia

What about you? What is your passion?

Is it the environment? Join the Sierra Club.

Is it world hunger? Food drives, food pantries, and soup kitchens need volunteers.

Is it health care? Blood drives need to be organized and health education lectures need to be coordinated.

Is it kids? Volunteer to gather gifts for underprivileged children or answer Dear Santa letters.

How about your hometown? Help your community stop developers from defacing the landscape with yet another shopping mall.

When you join a cause that you are passionate about, you're not thinking, "What do others think of me?" You are concentrating on, "What can all of us do for them?" When the goal is foremost in your mind, shyness fades into the background. A bond grows between people working for the same cause, and quality friendships form naturally.

ShyBuster #58
Find Your Passion and Purpose

Do some deep thinking on what causes you care about the most. Something you *really* care about. Then search the Internet and newspapers for groups or meetings on the subject. If your town has an alternative or underground paper, those are usually rich sources of a wide variety of organizations and meetings.

But don't join just anything. Find something you are fervent about and go for it. Let your passion drive your shyness out.

THE INCREDIBLE POWER OF PASSION NEVER ENDS

The power of passion is so mighty that, even after you become a certified Sure, it will help you achieve increasingly higher levels of confidence.

Even after I had claimed victory over shyness, for example, the thought of giving a speech turned my legs to linguine.

I once had a little company called Showtime at Sea. My partner, a wonderful gay man named Chip, and I produced entertainment for cruise ships. We had traveled the world together, and he was my closest and dearest friend.

Chip contracted AIDS, and I nursed him through a horrible and painful death. At his funeral, his sister asked if anyone wanted to say a few words. As three or four of his relatives stood and spoke about Chip's kind qualities, I realized that they knew nothing of his professional accomplishments. To them, he was just Jan and Nick's little boy, grown up.

I was unable to stay seated. My hand shot up like a rocket, and I almost dashed to the podium at the front of the funeral hall. I spoke passionately and unself-consciously for twenty minutes about what a talented, loving, and brilliant man Chip was.

It was the first time I'd ever stood in front of a group of people speaking. But not for one moment did I feel like I was giving a speech to a group. The mission was to inform Chip's extended family about his very special gifts.

I didn't think about it at the time, of course, but that experience was a big step in Graduated Exposure that contributed to my becoming a professional speaker who now speaks to large groups, sometimes up to ten thousand people.

Uncover your purpose. Your passion will help you achieve it without fear.

Eight Advanced, Sure-Fire Shy Extinguishers

Did you ever play the classic board game Monopoly? An unfortunate role of the dice meant "Do not pass Go, do not collect $200"–and then you landed in jail.

Nobody is going to put you in jail if you haven't succeeded with Shybusters #1-58. *But do not pass Go.* Go back to the beginning of *Good-Bye to Shy* and tick off the ShyBusters you have succeeded with. Then, you guessed it, you must master those remaining before continuing.

Starting here, we are delving into a wide variety of advanced techniques ranging from dares to dogs, buddies to bloopers, eating to acting, and shopping to listening to strange voices . . . and more.

These diverse ShyBusters only have one thing in common. They all work!

— • —

(43)

A Dare a Day Drives Shyness Away

Start by pulling out the lists you made in ShyBusters #16 and #17 in Part 3. In ShyBuster #16, you listed the situations that make your hands sweat, your heart quake, and your entire being want to vanish into thin air. Then, in ShyBuster #17, you sorted them from least intimidating to the most threatening.

Place your inventory of ordeals on one side of a desk or table. Put your date book on the other. Now assign yourself one of your personal challenges for each week–or a new one every few days for some of the easier ones. Naturally, you'll need to take into consideration which activities are feasible. Try explaining to your employer that you spent Tuesday at the spa because having massages made you nervous! Save that for your Saturday dare.

KICK IT UP A NOTCH

Each time you accomplish your goal, kick it up a notch to something "scarier" the next day. For example, if one of your biggest challenges is casually conversing with people, your assignment might look something like this.

Week one: Chat with people you know while riding in the elevator. When you're comfortable with that, initiate conversations with slight acquaintances. Then graduate to talking to strangers or a superior during the elevator ride.

Week two: Take walks after work and smile at people. It's obviously easy to smile at some people, while others are more intimidating. Gradually work your way up from giving a warm smile to curious toddlers to grinning at the most daunting-looking folks–maybe an attractive stranger you'd like to meet.

Week three: Join casual "watercooler" conversations at the office. After a couple of days of that, ask a colleague or two to join you for lunch.

Week four: Now you're up to asking strangers on the street directions or for the time. "Excuse me, could you tell me what time it is?" When you can do that with ease, start having longer chats with people in the ATM or grocery store line. Compliment them on something they are wearing or their cute kid. Does the woman in the produce aisle have one of those strange-looking Asian vegetables in her basket? Ask her what it is and how to cook it.

Week five: Speak up in office meetings. When that becomes more relaxed, introduce a new subject in a meeting.

Week six: Call someone of the opposite sex, but not necessarily someone you are attracted to. Ask that "other-gendered" person to join you for some social activity. Women, it's the twenty-first century. You can do that, too!

When you are ready, of course, kick it up the last notch to calling someone you are attracted to. If you are married or already-partnered, you be the one to pick up the phone and invite another couple to dinner.

By scheduling daily challenges, you are generating a personalized G.E.T. program, the most effective shyness-zapper in existence.

ShyBuster #59
Design Your Own "Dare-a-Day" Program

Assign yourself one challenge weekly from your ShyBuster #16 list of intimidating situations. Then split it into daily assignments and do each one in order.

If you're not satisfied with your performance, slot your daily dare in a second time. And a third and a fourth—until you've licked it. Shys, do not skip this one. It is crucial to your goal of being shy-free.

Hint: It's human nature to find a reason not to do something. No excuses allowed! To make it more difficult to weasel out of your daily dare, tell a friend or family member what you're up to and report to them daily.

(44)

Take a Bite Out of Shyness for Lunch

A VERY HEALTHY DIET

A shy-busting exercise that you can practice at the same time each day is extremely effective. What better time than lunch hour? Every midday, take on an additional tiny challenge.

Suppose that you eat lunch every day at the company cafeteria. Your date book might look something like this:

Monday: Stop in the cafeteria in the morning and ask what today's lunch special will be.
Tuesday: Talk longer with the employees in the cafeteria. Tell them how much you liked yesterday's pumpkin pie and ask whether they'll be having it again. Tell one of them that some-day you'd like to get the recipe for their salad dressing. Ask if you can substitute mashed potatoes for the corn. And so on.
Wednesday: Stop by a colleague's table and ask if he recommends the ham sandwich he's eating.
Thursday: Invite someone to sit with you in the cafeteria.
Friday: Ask if you can join several people you know at a table.

The possibilities are endless. So are the benefits. But you must keep up the routine. It's like bodybuilding, which is graduated exposure to heavier and heavier weights. Do a heavy workout occasionally and you'll break your back. Do a light workout every day and you'll soon be lifting back-breaking weight effortlessly.

Likewise, if you attempt big challenges all at once, you can break your confidence. Take on a light challenge every day and you'll soon be throwing your own weight around smoothly. Forgive my repeating it, but almost every mental health professional agrees that G.E.T. is the most potent shyness extinguisher.

ShyBuster #60
Eat Your Shyness at Lunch

Give yourself a tiny lunchtime assignment each day. And, as always, go from the simplest to the scariest tasks.

To make sure you'll follow through, punish yourself if you don't attempt it. Let's say that your challenge du jour was to invite someone to join you. Make a rule. You don't do it, you don't eat. You'll be amazed at what an effective motivation hunger is.

Shop 'til You . . . Stamp Out Shyness

I'M JUST LOOKING

Interacting with salespeople is a super way to practice your social skills (not to mention fun for you shopaholics!). Retail people standing behind their counters are just waiting to talk to potential customers. So take advantage of the free practice and ask for their help—lots of help—as you browse through a store.

I hate shopping because I'm always embarrassed to tell the salesperson I'm just looking. I feel so guilty if they show me a few things and I leave not even buying one. I buy a lot of things by mail order but I don't like it because a lot of things don't fit and I have to send them back. But at least the mail order people don't know me.

–Pamela G., Tulsa, Oklahoma

I e-mailed Pamela and begged her not to feel guilty. I told her—and I'll tell you, too—that salespeople really don't expect you to buy. On the average, only one in twenty people who look at a product actually reaches for their wallet. Additionally, many salespeople are not working on commission and thus really don't care whether they make the sale.

Even if you do intend to purchase an item and you know precisely which one, ask the clerk to show you the others. Then ask for recommendations.

You think that the clerk will be ever-so-slightly offended if you don't take the one she suggested? Perhaps a tad, but that is excellent practice in standing up for your choices.

ShyBuster #61
Be a Shopaholic—Who Doesn't Buy

Set aside a few evenings and weekends to go shopping. Many mall crawlers go just for the pleasure of it and never buy a thing—so don't feel obligated to purchase anything. Chat with the salespeople. Ask for recommendations. Then, when you feel more comfortable, buy something— then return it the next day. Now you're really taking shyness by the horns. Remember, a salesclerk's frown never killed anyone.

Let Man's Best Friend Lend You a Paw

A NEW TWIST ON TRITE BUT TRUE ADVICE

Of course, chatting with strangers is an excellent confidence builder. But wouldn't it be easier if you didn't have to make the approach? And wouldn't it be even lovelier if admiring passersby approached you with a smile, a compliment, and some questions that you're an expert on?

I'm sure you've been deluged with advice and, no doubt, "get a dog" is near the top of the list. But here is where you surpass that hackneyed recommendation. Choose an unusual canine. That way when people stop you on the street, as they inevitably will, you can regale them with stories of your "best friend's" history and heritage, a subject you'll soon be expert at.

GET A LOOK-ALIKE DOG

Even better, get a dog that matches your appearance or your personality. "What?" you rightfully ask.

Seriously, there is inexplicable charm to the combo of you and your (sort-of) look-alike pooch. I'll never forget a striking woman I once saw walking an Afghan hound down Fifth Avenue in New York City. Both her and her dog's cashmere-colored hair were fluttering in the wind. (It didn't hurt that Afghan hounds have widely spaced hip joints, which make their derrieres swing like a model sashaying down the runway.)

Women, of course you want a stylish bitch (relax, the "b" word simply means "female dog"). Like the Afghan's owner, try to have your canine's hair color be similar to yours. People can't help but admire (even if they don't tell you) the similar shade in both your tresses.

Men, forget French poodles or other powder-puff pooches. Depending on your appearance, go with a dalmatian or Doberman pincher. If you're short, you can't go wrong with a mean-looking bulldog, the champion of pit fighting. (As masculine though it may seem, avoid the pit bull. It will have the opposite effect–of making strangers run from you.)

Of course, some bizarre breed dogs cost a lot. Forget the costliest ones because there are thousands of fabulous, funny-looking mutts at the pound. You'll be doing the canine world a favor by choosing one that nobody else has chosen–and giving yourself a new best friend besides.

ShyBuster #62
Attention-Getter on a Leash

Men, walking a manly mutt on a chain can do wonders for your masculinity. Women, a chic canine on a quality leash makes you look all the lovelier to passersby.

Prepare yourself with some engrossing small talk about your pooch. Then leave it to the admiring strangers to approach you for small talk.

(47)

Blooper Therapy

THE CHICKEN LITTLE SYNDROME

Let's say Ms. Shy is lunching with office colleagues at a restaurant to welcome several new employees. She hesitates at the doorway. *Shall I shake hands with them? Where should I sit if no one indicates my chair? Where should I put my purse?* More imagined calamities come to mind: *What if I spill my water and everyone looks at me? What if I mispronounce somebody's name? What if I sit in the wrong place?* What if . . . ? What if . . .? What if . . .?

Do you remember the story of Chicken Little, who swore that the sky was falling just because one acorn landed on her head? Unfortunately, some Shys are like that. If they are unsure of one little social convention, they fear that they'll do all the wrong things, at the wrong time, in the wrong way—in every social situation.[33]

But here is extraordinary news: You probably know precisely what to do in practically all situations. You just think that you don't. In one study, researchers asked Shys how they would handle a variety of difficult social circumstances.[34] Their shy subjects surprised the researchers with their cool, calm, and correct answers.

The Shy who wondered if she should shake hands would answer, "Well, I suppose I'd look around to see if other arrivals are shaking hands." Right!

Researcher: "What if you should spill your water?"

Ms. Shy: "I guess I'd mop it up as unobtrusively as possible."
Right!

Researcher: "What if you mispronounce somebody's name?"

Ms. Shy: "Well, I'd probably just say 'excuse me' and continue on with what I was saying." Right!

Even if you know the correct answer (and you probably do!), panic prevents you from thinking of it at the instant the mishap happens. As your spilled drink streams toward a colleague's lap, you probably feel like you're tied to your chair by political enemies. With blindingly bright lights shining in your eyes, they pummel you with questions on how to handle the spilled-drink catastrophe.

That's the condition. What's the remedy?

WRITE A HORROR STORY

I'm sure that you are aware that visualization is not just used by sports psychologists to get their clients to go for the gold. It can also help you do the coolest thing when social disaster strikes.

Let's say you must attend a business dinner.

Step One: Before you leave, write a horror story of all of the ways you could possibly make an utter fool of yourself. *What if I burp audibly? What if I break a glass? What if I spill my soup?*

Step Two: Upon finishing your frightening list, ask yourself what someone *should* do after burping, breaking, or spilling. When you think about it *unemotionally*, you know precisely how to handle it.

Step Three: Close your eyes and "see" yourself making the blooper. Then visualize yourself taking precisely the action that you came up with. Continue this visualization process with each disaster until you've chased all of the butterflies away.

Now, in the remote possibility that the tragedy does transpire, you don't need to suffer the horror of "What do I do now?" Thanks to your previous visualization, your body will go on autopilot and you will sail through the situation with panache.

All gold medal swimmers, runners, and lugers visualize themselves coming in first amidst the roaring crowd and frenzied TV reporters. Visualization. If it works for Olympic athletes, it will work for you.

ShyBuster #63
Make a Mental Movie of Yourself
Handling Goof-Ups with Grace

Think of all of the horrendously humiliating situations that could possibly happen to you in a social situation. Then, with a cool head, look at each scene and ask yourself what somebody *should* do in that situation. Nine times out of ten, you'll be right on target. Now visualize yourself responding to each situation exactly as you've planned. The ghost of Amy Vanderbilt will give you a standing ovation. And you'll be prepared for whatever comes your way.

"I HAVEN'T A CLUE WHAT TO DO"

Inevitably, of course, situations will arise where neither a Sure nor a Shy would spontaneously know what to do. Let's say that you drop your fork at a dinner party. Those nasty inner voices taunt you.

Hey, butterfingers, pick the darn thing up.

C'mon, haven't you got any class? Call the waiter.

Stupid, that would only call attention to your blooper. Let it lie there.

Wait a minute, just kick it under the table so nobody sees it. Then finish your roast beef with your spoon.

While fantasizing these humiliating horrors, someone spots the frozen hysteria on your face and turns toward you. "Is anything wrong?" they ask. Now you want to die.

I once faced that very same fork predicament. It plopped right under my chair. I knew it would look ridiculous eating peas with my spoon so, not knowing what to do, I didn't eat another morsel. When I got home, munching on a sandwich, I pulled a dusty Amy Vanderbilt etiquette book off the shelf–written in 1956. Eureka! On a page yellowed with age, I found the answer. (It's option two–call the waiter and ask for a replacement fork.)

Until you become a certified Sure and trust your own instincts, an etiquette book covers most possible social catastrophes. I know that the word *etiquette* sounds stuffy. But the books are no longer just "What should the mother of the bride wear?" or "What kind of personal stationary should I have?" My favorite, *Miss Manner's Guide for the Turn of the Millennium*, has chapters like "How Not to Stand Around Looking Stupid."[35]

Guys, don't skip this one. It's for you, too. (Or, should I say, *especially* for you?)

ShyBuster #64
Read What Manners Mavens Say

Read a good etiquette book. It's great preparation for facing dreadful dilemmas like "what do I do when a tabletop tsunami from my coffee cup heads her way?" With the confidence of knowing what the experts suggest, your anxiety evaporates. You won't worry that the Etiquette Police will come to arrest you–or worse, that people will laugh at you.

The Confidence "Stage"

SEE LIGHT AT THE END OF THE TUNNEL

After using most of the ShyBusters we've discussed, I felt the dark cloud of agonizing shyness slowly lifting. In addition to the ShyBusters, my "coffee, tea, or me" people job (pampering hundreds of airline passengers weekly for two years) helped a lot.

Even though I could see the light at the end of the tunnel, I craved one more professional "clash with crowds" to confirm that I was "cured" forever. For two summers, I took a job as a social hostess on a cruise ship. (To get my coveted job, I used ShyBuster #19, the wacko morning workout to pump my energy level sky-high before walking through each interviewer's door. Then, as ShyBuster #38 directs, I interviewed with four other cruise ship lines before I went for the one I wanted.)

As the ship's social hostess, it was my job to hold a singles get-together at every departure. After the confetti settled on the deck and the waving well-wishers on the shore disappeared in the distance, I'd welcome the singles into the disco. Every week I saw the guys grin and the girls glower when they realized that the female-to-male ratio on a ship is three to one. (Women, if you go on a cruise, don't expect the love boat. Men, it's the love boat.) Immediately the women would begin to descend on the few men like vultures on a lamb chop.

IT TAKES ONE TO SPOT ONE

At one such get-together, they missed one fellow sitting alone in the corner. I went to greet him, and he gave a hesitant hello at a volume a librarian would approve of. Most people don't instantly recognize a Shy, but, as one who has fought the bitter battle, I saw shyness written all over him.

I knew there wasn't much I could do for Ned in one week, but I wanted to give it a try. I invited him to have coffee on deck with me the next morning. He seemed more at ease when I told him about my successful struggle with shyness. He told me that he was thinking of taking speech classes because his voice was so weak.

When I was in high school, I, too, thought that would help. It just so happened that my mother was a speech therapist, one of the best in the country I might brag. I asked Mama for speech lessons to help me learn to speak up and not sound so shy.

She told me speech lessons wouldn't help. She was right. Research has subsequently shown that speech lessons are not the right path.[36] There is a more direct road to having a smooth, strong, and confident voice. In fact, it's a superhighway.

"Ned, may I suggest a way that has been proven far more effective?" I attentively asked.

He looked at me skeptically. "What is it?"

I told him.

"I'll think it over," he mumbled.

On Saturday, the cruise was over. I said good-bye to the passengers and gave Ned a hug as he headed down the gangplank.

"Ned, stay in touch!" I called after him.

I didn't expect to hear from Ned again, but the first time we docked in New York the following summer, the steward delivered a dozen roses to my cabin. The card read "Love from Ned, your shy passenger from last year. Can you meet me on the dock? I have some exciting news."

I descended the gangplank, planning to search for my timid friend hovering at the edge of the crowd. Above the clamor of the crowd, however, I heard, "Leil, Leil, over here." An energetic fellow waving both arms came running toward the ship.

"Ned?" I gasped. This lively guy couldn't be nervous Ned.

HAMMING IT UP WORKS

Sitting at the coffee shop at the port, he told me that he had taken my suggestion of acting classes seriously. He'd been in three shows already and now was playing the role of the obnoxious, loudmouthed Stanley in *A Streetcar Named Desire.* Imagining Ned on stage in his T-shirt, slapping a beer on the table and hollering for his wife, was mind-boggling.

"Leil," he said, "it is amazing." He told me that he learned to project his voice to the last row. He told me how he learned to make big gestures. "That and making eye contact with all of the performers was a life changer." Ned looked exuberant. "If I can take on three distinct personalities for an audience of 100, I can take on the role of 'confident person' for a mere twenty or so people at a party."

One of the things that I think really helped my shyness was when my best friend joined the drama club at school and wanted me to join, too. We did some scenes and in one of them I was cast as this very flashy outgoing lady. I was scared to death at first but, after having that personality on stage, it was a little easier to exert myself in real life.

−Alisa L., Washington, D.C.

"IS THAT REALLY ME?"

I was thrilled for Ned and have subsequently suggested acting lessons to students in my shyness seminars. Sometimes they protest, "But if I were just pretending to be an extroverted person off stage, it wouldn't be really 'me.'"

At first, of course, you won't feel like the old shy you. But isn't that what you're trying to escape? You want to become the new confident you.

While acting, you will still be yourself in all of the important ways—your beliefs, your values, your principles. You will simply have the personality and confidence to speak up more often and in a stronger voice so that people listen. As one study counsels, "Shy people are often concerned whether or not their actions reflect their real selves. Like a method actor, you must learn to dissolve the bond between the so-called real you and the role you play."[37]

A famous comedian, actress, singer, and dancer who was painfully shy confirms this, crediting acting as the breakthrough for her:

Being able to step out of yourself and into a role, a character behind a mask of anonymity, enables a basically shy person to perform in person.

–Carol Burnett

ShyBuster #65
Act Your Way to Confidence

Being somebody else on stage does wonders for playing the most important role of your life—your most confident self. Take an acting class. After using larger movements, a louder voice, and good eye contact on stage, you'll be just as dynamic at the last night closing party—and in many more social situations to come.

Fast Audiotrack to Confidence

DOWNLOAD CONFIDENCE INTO YOUR EARDRUMS

While driving, do you have lyrics like these running through your head?

I acted so shy. I know everybody noticed.

I didn't know anybody there. I just stood around looking like an idiot.

It was horrible. I couldn't even look him in the eyes.

I can't ask her for a date. She'd laugh at me.

Some Shys, in an attempt to tune out the criticism of their inner voices, roll up the windows and turn the radio volume up to earsplitting. They figure it will take their concentration off themselves. By the second song, however, it just becomes background noise for their destructive self-talk.

TURN OFF THE MUSIC, TURN ON THE CONFIDENCE

You've heard the saying "Fight fire with fire." Well, the only way to fight these voices is with other voices. Millions of positive voices in the form of audio programs are just waiting to enter your ears and drive negative thoughts out.

Recently, instead of playing music in my car, I put in some of those CDs where someone is talking about positive things. My favorite, of course, is your "Conversation Confidence," then Brian Tracy's "The Psychology of Sales." It's been very helpful on my job, but most important, it keeps my mind off myself except for planning to do some of the positive and profitable stuff you and Tracy suggest.

–Will H., Chicago, Illinois

It was kind of Will to mention my communications audio, but I also suggest listening to programs that have nothing to do with confidence or social skills. Find an audio program on how to fix your car, feng shui your home, or get rid of clutter–the list is endless. In addition to learning new skills, every audio you listen to makes you a more interesting person and gives you more to talk about.

ShyBuster #66
Listen to Positive Voices in Your Car

Thousands of audio programs are sitting on library or store shelves. Or hiding on the Internet, waiting to be downloaded into your ears while driving, jogging, or just strolling around town. These programs push punishing self-thoughts out and pump interesting ideas in. Start a healthy mental diet to replace poisonous thinking.

Don't forget the plethora of audio fiction, which can fill your mind with engrossing stories to replace the horror stories of your imagined screw-ups.

10

Sex and the Single Shy

One would think that sex could be a problem for Shys. And, for some who have performance problems, it can be. However only a small percentage of Shys have difficulties with sex.[38] *It is getting the right partner that is the challenge.*

Shys have a greater need to connect with someone because they are more sensitive.[39] Shys often are more intense about their love relationships, so there can be complications.[40]

Shy people typically wed later than those who are not shy or anxious around other people.[41]

–British Journal of Psychiatry

Single Shys, here I will share a few "must dos" with you to help you find the right partner for you. Those of you who have read my book *How to Make Anyone Fall in Love with You* may recognize several of the techniques, which are now tweaked for shy seekers of love. I will also help you develop your own lover's Graduated Exposure Therapy program to make you more comfortable in the dating scene.

——— • ———

The Lovin' Is Easy—It's the Gettin' There That's Hard

Several years ago, I volunteered for a charity event with an Indian woman named Aastha. She and I became quite close and, during our long hours together, talked about everything imaginable–including her sex life.

Aastha had been recently married. I asked her how she had met her husband. "Steven was in a drawing class I was taking," she told me. He never talked to anybody. She smiled. "I thought he was sort of cute, so I said 'hi' to him once. He didn't say anything but I know he was pleased.

"During the next couple of classes we exchanged a few words. Then a Modigliani exhibition came to town. I wanted to see it and asked if he would join me.

"He did. One thing led to another and we started dating." Aastha smiled again. "The rest is history." She lowered her voice. "He is still shy around people, but he sure isn't shy about one thing." She looked around to make sure no one was listening. "He is unbelievable!" There was no doubt what she was talking about.

If Aastha had not made the first move, she and Steven would not be a couple today.

I realized that if my wife wasn't the aggressive type, we would never have been together. We were set up on a blind date. I golfed with a man whose wife worked with my now wife. Our first kiss was entirely my wife's instigation. While I was attracted to her, if she hadn't made it so blatantly clear that she liked me, I probably would have assumed she didn't and never bothered calling her again.

–David D., Great Falls, Montana

THERE ARE NO LOVE "GUARANTEES"

There is one book, more than any other, that is literally within arm's reach of most psychiatrists and psychologists. It is the *Diagnostic and Statistical Manual of Mental Disorders*–the psychiatry "Bible," as some call it. Whenever a question comes up, their hands shoot across the desk. With a quick flip of the pages, they find the answer to almost any psychological question–such as why finding a partner is more difficult for Shys than for the rest of the population.

> Shy people are hypersensitive to potential rejection, humiliation, or shame. Social avoidants are unwilling to enter into situations unless given unusually strong guarantees of uncritical acceptance.[42]
>
> –*Diagnostic and Statistical Manual of Mental Disorders*

On your first date, you can't say to someone, "If we have a second date, do you promise to love me and be faithful to me forever?" Yet that is what many Shys subconsciously want.

Intellectually, of course, we know there are no "guarantees" in love for Shys. (Nor for the Sures, nor even for the rich or famous. Especially the last category!) However, practically all Shys are capable of falling in love, being deeply loved by their partners, and having a lifelong, fulfilling relationship.

SOME GOOD NEWS ABOUT SHYS AND LOVE

The good news is that when you do find a partner, you are usually capable of a deeper dedication than non-Shys. If the love is carefully controlled and reciprocated, it can bring both partners manifold pleasures that are often out of the reach of Sures who have dated extensively and had more love relationships.

Additionally, when you are in a good relationship, your partner will appreciate some of your more sensitive qualities.

> When [highly sensitive] Shys finally do find their life partner, their spouses usually highly appreciate their qualities. Husbands and wives of Shys described their spouses' qualities as "modest," "cautious," "dignified," "sensitive," "mannerly," and "sincere."[43]
>
> –SHYNESS: PERSPECTIVES ON RESEARCH AND TREATMENT

SHYS FALL HARD AND FAST

Why do Shys fall in love more intensely than non-Shys?[44] It is because many of them draw a thick protective ring around their inner lives. When someone *does* crash through that circle, he or she becomes particularly precious. Some Shys love their partner as much as or more than themselves.

Why quicker? Because they don't usually date a lot and, when someone they are crazy about responds, whammo! They can be quick to take the fall.

Here are some questions you might want to ask yourself:

- Does my intense need for love stem from lack of self-esteem?
- Am I tempted to fall in love with the first person who says "I love you"?
- Do I need a partner to feel "complete"?

- Would I fall so deeply in love that it could suffocate my partner?
- Could my relationship be shaky because I might be too shy to socialize or do things with my partner?
- Would I be haunted by fears and fantasies of my partner's safety or infidelity?

If you answered a lot of yeses, you have some homework to do. First, recognize how vulnerable you might be, which can have dire consequences on your relationships. Then concentrate on annihilating unhealthy thoughts. You do that in the same way you destroy the other destructive thoughts we talked about in Part 2. Only then can you comfortably progress with the following ShyBusters to find the right partner.

ShyBuster #67
Give Yourself an Emotional Checkup

As you begin your search for love, ask yourself the serious questions listed above. "Yes" answers can be symptoms of emotional neediness. Ponder these questions—and your answers—carefully, because Shys are more prone to love problems.[45]

To recap, it is more difficult for you, as a Shy, to find a good relationship. And, when you do, there are potential perils. But if you take extra care to circumvent the problems, your previous anguish can be counterbalanced by incomparable bliss. You can experience intense joy in your relationship that a number of Sures never find!

BEING SHY AND GAY IS LONELY

A reader named Paul reminded me of the significant number of gay people who are also shy, lonely, and seeking love. Thank you, Paul, for your gentle chiding and for your very poignant letter.

I have a tremendous lack of self-esteem that has plagued me for many years. I know I must improve upon my self-confidence. First, I want to tell you that your books and recordings have changed my life. I find myself agreeing with you often, constantly seeing myself and my problems and faux pas in your stories and descriptions. However, in that search to improve, I find I have to chart my own course even more so than many of your readers. I wanted to let you know with the hopes that you might think a little about how to address my problems and those of millions of other people.

You see—and I'd be surprised if you hadn't guessed this already—I'm gay. I'm a forty-two-year-old male, who for the most part of his life has been unable to find a partner or even very many people to date. I know many people think most gay men don't have a big problem in relating to other gay men. And you may even have the impression that gay life is just hopping from one bed to another—or from one partner to another. But this isn't true for a lot of us—especially the older people and people not raised in big cities or the more progressive areas of the country. I'd venture to guess that even though probably 10 percent of the population is gay or bi, we need help in figuring out how to find a good partner.

As wonderful as your books and CDs are, they are structured to the heterosexual side of the equation. I do understand that's what you are and it constitutes the majority of your readers. And I certainly wouldn't ask you to put out a series targeting gays (and/or lesbians, and all the other colors in the diverse rainbow).

But please, consider letting your readers know that we feel the same way, and have even greater challenges because we are gay. I know I'm not the only shy gay out here—and we need the help as much as anyone else. Especially the gay man or woman in smaller towns and rural areas who may not be able to find counselors or therapists who can or will deal with gays. And many gays consider themselves isolated and friendless and are in need of help when it comes to personal relationship skills.

Most of the gays I know and chat with online, both in the United States and throughout the world, really do want to find someone to love who loves us back. And someone who wants to be in a long-term relationship. I'm sure I'm not the only gay male in the United States who doesn't want to grow old alone.

—Paul M., Dallas, Texas

I'd like underscore that, although I use gender-specific language in *Good-Bye to Shy*, all of the ShyBusters are for same-sex love as well.

English is a bulky language and all writers struggle with the words *he* and *she* when either could be correct. I also find that reading *potential love partner* too often becomes ponderous. Linguistically, gender-specific words flow more smoothly. Words like *opposite sex*, although often not appropriate, are part of our language. Please understand that when I use these words, it is merely for linguistic simplicity. I am hoping that our language changes to encompass everyone—not to mention to make it easier for us writers!

No Lookin', No Lovin'

As a recovered Shy, I am now a relentless people watcher. Whether in an airport, in a Starbucks, or at a gathering, my eyes sweep the room like an electronic scanner silently scrutinizing people interacting with each other. Sadly, I see a heartbreaking human drama reenacted literally hundreds of times in hundreds of places.

A man's and a woman's eyes meet. You can almost hear their harmony. For them, the music is swelling and strains of "Our Love Is Here to Stay" fill the room.

But he's shy and quickly looks away, pretending he's not the least bit interested. She's timid, too, and inspects the floor for dust. Inevitably, after about thirty seconds, she risks a brisk peek to see if he's still looking at her. But alas, out of timidity, his eyes are elsewhere. Another half minute passes and, puffing up both his courage and his chest, he hazards another look. But alas, she is gone.

If only one of them had the courage to look at the other and smile, millions of scenes like this would have happier endings.

I am petrified of even looking at attractive women. I know that if I fall in love that I would be so vulnerable. She could walk all over me and I would just lie down and say "walk harder." I would lose total control.

Because of this, I don't even look at women I'm attracted to. I hate what I'm doing but I can't stop it. It scares me that I may be missing a lot of chances for a meaningful relationship.

–Don G., Lindenhurst, New York

ALL FOR THE WANT OF A SMILE

You've heard, "For the want of a nail, a shoe was lost; for the want of a shoe, a horse was lost; for the want of a horse, a rider was lost; for the want of a rider, a battle was lost; for the want of a battle, a kingdom was lost. All for the want of a nail!"

Just as true is: For the want of a smile, a conversation was lost. For the want of conversation, a date was lost. For the want of a date, a love was lost. For the want of love, a lifetime of happiness together was lost. All for the want of a smile.

Smile and say "hello." It could change your life.

Smiling at an attractive potential partner is one of the biggest challenges for a Shy. Few singles–Shy or Sure–understand that the second someone spots you and finds you attractive, he or she wonders whether you are open to communicating with him or her. Because even Sures fear rejection, you must let that potential partner know that the answer is "yes" by smiling at him or her.

For Men Only

Men, let's start with you. You spot a woman you like. You've rehearsed your smile enough in the mirror to know how your warm and friendly smile feels. Now, take a deep breath, soften your face, and give her one of your finest.

Please understand that if she looks away, it definitely does not mean that she isn't interested. Females from the dawn of civilization have been taught to flutter their eyelashes and look away. To women, that is flirting.

But *you*, gentlemen, must not look away. Even in the famous painting depicting the beginning of time, "The Fall of Man: Adam and Eve," Adam is gazing directly into Eve's eyes. But she is demurely looking away–even while enticing him with the forbidden apple!

It's almost a law of nature that women modestly (or strategically) look away when your eyes meet theirs. Shys, don't be deterred. Employ

ShyBuster #9, "Reject Imagined Rejection." The world's most eligible bachelor could glance at a woman, and her eyes would flutter away to the floor.

Now here is where it gets interesting. Dr. Timothy Perper spent years researching courtship patterns. His laboratory? A singles bar. A man looks at a woman. Perper discovered that if she is interested in him, she will first look away and then look up again within forty-five seconds. Not only that, gentlemen, but you can judge if she is responsive by *how* she looks away.[46]

If your eyes are elsewhere when she looks up again, the budding relationship could crash. Instead, keep your eyes in her direction and, when she looks up the second time, grace the woman with your warm smile again. I'd place bets that her reaction will be a lot warmer this time.

Your next move is to approach her and (no "pickup lines," *please!*) either introduce yourself or ask her an innocuous question to get small talk started.

ShyBuster #68
Men, Smile Twice at Attractive Women

Smile at a woman you are attracted to—*twice!* Understand that she has been trained since she was sitting on daddy's lap to demurely look away when a man smiles at her. Unless the woman is totally turned off, she not only welcomes but also expects a second smile.

For Women Only

Shy ladies, even in the twenty-first century, most women believe that men must make the first move in initiating a relationship. Not true! In a study called "Nonverbal Courtship Patterns in Women: Context and

Consequences," researchers filmed a singles party with hidden cameras in the ceiling.[47] When viewing the videotape afterward, they discovered that men didn't usually approach a woman unless she had given him a subtle nonverbal invitation. The most common signal? A simple smile.

Surprised and fascinated by these findings, the researchers then surveyed hundreds of steadily dating and married couples. Much to their amazement, in two-thirds of all relationships, they discovered that the woman had smiled, sent an even more obvious signal, or spoken to her partner first. In other words, she started the ball rolling.

Of course, smiling at a desirable man isn't easy. But take courage in the fact that, due to his male ego, he probably won't even remember that you gave him a nonverbal signal to lure him over. He will give himself the credit!

ShyBuster #69
Women, Smile First at Attractive Men

Smile at every attractive man you see. It gets progressively easier. That way, when you see *the* man who makes your heart feel like a jackhammer at full throttle, you won't freeze. You'll be able to lure him over with your "come-hither" smile.

My shyness was much worse with men that I was interested in dating. I had a crush on two guys at my gym but could not make direct eye contact or even talk to them. I even went to a bookstore to read up on how to flirt or talk to them. I did my research and picked the day to make conversation. When the day came, I choked. I just could not get past my crippling shyness, I was terrified. I was so frustrated and upset at my inability to talk to them that I went home and cried . . . a lot.

—Dina B., Topeka, Kansas

FLIRTATIOUS EYE CONTACT

One thing is sure. Without eye contact, love and desire do not develop. With minimal eye contact, it could. With extra-long eye contact, you increase your chances astronomically.

First, you must be absolutely convinced of how crucial elongated eye contact is to love. A study called "Looking and Loving: The Effects of Mutual Gaze on Feelings of Romantic Love" proved that men and women who had extended eye contact during a casual conversation developed "significantly higher feelings of affection than subjects who had less eye contact with each other."[48]

Why? Anthropologist Helen Fisher tells us that it is basic animal instinct.[49] Unyielding eye contact creates a highly emotional state similar to fear. When you look directly and potently into someone's eyes, his or her body actually produces a chemical similar to adrenalin, which creates the same tingly sensation that people feel when falling in love—and lust!

Psychologists studying love often use a gauge called Rubin's Scale, which determines people's feelings for each other. The prominent psychologist who devised it, Zick Rubin, conducted a study called "Measurement of Romantic Love."[50] He found that people who were deeply in love gaze intently at each other for a much longer time than normal. When strangers are conversing, they look at each other on the average only 30 to 60 percent of the time. Confident and comfortable lovers increase that to 75 percent.

I won't promise that flirting with your eyes is going to be painless at first. But it will not be terrifying if (and only if!) you have practiced your eye contact exercises, ShyBusters #22, 23, and 24. If you haven't, go back and master those first. Otherwise, you risk failing at flirting and will become discouraged.

If you do find eye contact difficult, make sure to use ShyBuster #26, silently saying, "I like you" while keeping your eyes on the other person's.

"I REALLY, REALLY, REALLY, REALLY, REALLY, REALLY LIKE YOU"

Now you go for the big stakes. The following ShyBuster makes your eyes inviting and sensual. Although it works for both sexes, it is even more potent when a man looks into a woman's eyes this way.

When saying hello to an attractive someone of the opposite sex, extend the silent "I like you" to:

"I really like you."

Then "I really, really like you."

Then "I really, really, really like you."

Then "I really, really, really, really like you."

When you've reached six "reallys," you have achieved some serious sensuous eye contact. You can tell by his or her slightly nervous but excited reaction.

Those extra seconds of eye contact speak silent volumes. Whether you are spotting a potential partner across the room or casually chatting with them, your extra eye contact exudes powerful romantic signals.

ShyBuster #70
Employ the "Really, Really, Really, Really" Flirtatious Eyes Technique

To help get yourself into extended eye contact when spotting a potential special other, silently say, "I really like you," then "I really, really like you"—and so on until you reach six "reallys." Soon you'll be able to give sensuous eye contact to the man or woman who used to make your throat feel like sandpaper and your hands drip like faucets.

Once you are in a relationship, change that "like" to "love." Can you imagine the effect your eyes have on your partner while silently saying, "I love you. I really, really, really, really, really, really love you"?

Relationship Rehearsals

"IT'S A JUNGLE OUT THERE"

As we all know, the dating scene can be pretty brutal. Even Sures say "it's a jungle out there" and it's survival of the (emotionally) fittest. Answer these mind-boggling questions.

Men, what is the difference between a beautiful woman and one who is, shall we say, "beauty challenged"?

Answer: One is beautiful, and one is not.

Women, what's the difference between a prince of a man and a frog of a fellow?

Answer: One's a prince of a man, and the other is a frog of a fellow.

Here's a question for both sexes: Why should you be nervous on a date with the first if not the second?

Answer: It's because we assume that desirable people are "different." But the truth is, they are not.

Men especially think that beautiful women are an exotic species. Not true. Having worked around beautiful women as a Pan Am flight attendant and during a mercifully brief time as a model, I know it's not. Everyone is lonely inside and wants to find the right someone.

All over the world, a beautiful woman can turn a dignified man into a dyslexic octopus. A businessman from Moscow wrote to me:

I must say I am usually most confident with women. However, I developed an interest in a stunning young lady who worked in a shoe store near my office. I would see her each evening through the window as I went home. Several times she smiled at me and I always thought to myself, when I finally meet her, what would I say? I prepared my poetic opening lines, my smooth Romeo approach, and my stunning Leo gaze. I imagined her responses, and how I would smoothly navigate through them to finally ask her out on a date. Well, it all seemed just fine and dandy until I actually went in to say hello. My speech stumbled, my palms got sweaty, and my words magically started missing syllables. She thought it was cute that my face turned red, and how I knocked down the entire display of women's shoes at her store. I quickly left and now walk around the block to avoid passing her store.

–Boris Z., Moscow, Russia

So how do you become more relaxed around top-notch potential partners? You do "dry run dates" with people who, for you personally, are romantic (forgive the phrase) "duds."

PRACTICE DATES MAKE (FUTURE) PERFECT DATES

Please, dear readers, forgive me if this sounds callous. Men, there are plenty of women who don't interest you, but who are dying to go out with you. Simply open your eyes and see which women are smiling at you, which women come to talk to you–in short, which women might say "YES!" if you asked them out.

Then reward one lucky woman next week. Take her to a nice restaurant, compliment her, and ask her questions about her life. Get practice–tasting the wine, putting her coat around her shoulders, offering your arm as you walk to the car. Not only is it a rehearsal for taking out a stunner, but you are doing a very nice thing for Plain Jane.

This is, of course, Graduated Exposure to more and more desirable women. Needless to say, you will be far more comfortable when you do ask the woman of your choice if you could have the pleasure of her company.

Likewise, women, the pond is full of frogs you wouldn't want as a life partner. But give the boys a thrill and go out with a few of them as "practice dates." If they don't ask, you ask them. The old rules are in a free fall.

Next smile and flirt with someone a bit more intimidating. Repeat this sequence until you are finally confident around Most Desired Male.

Ladies and gentlemen, I only ask you one favor. Please be gentle and loving with the feelings of your "stepping-stone dates." Enjoy your time together, even if you view it as practice, and be considerate of their feelings when you're ready to move on.

It seems that only losers ask me out and I don't want to waste my time with them. I really think I deserve better. Anyway, there is this man, Carl, I sort of had a crush on even though we had seldom spoken. He works on the eighteenth floor of my office building and I work on the twentieth. I think he liked me because he used to smile at me whenever he saw me. Carl happened to get into the elevator one time when I was riding down and I didn't know what to say to him. I work in a tall building so it was a very long ride. At the time, it seemed forever. He smiled at me and said, "You're very quiet today." I hate it when people say that.

I just looked down and then he said, "Are you shy?" I wanted to tell him no, but I was so nervous I couldn't. He then said some friends and their dates were going to the game that weekend and would I join him. I wanted so much to say yes but I'd never been to a football game and I wouldn't know how to act. The elevator reached the ground just then and I can't believe I just ran out the door. It was horrible—I can hardly face him at work anymore and he doesn't smile at me anymore.

–Laurel H., Smyrna, Delaware

Laurel, it sounds as though you could have gone to a football game with any number of those men you call "losers" just for the experience. Even frogs speak football. Learning how to jump up and down and yell for their team would have probably made you confident enough to say "yes" to Carl.

ShyBuster #71
Practice "Practice Dating"

Start dating some people you are not intimidated by or even personally attracted to. Get comfortable with making the approach, asking or hinting for the date, wearing the clothing, conversing, flirting, dancing, ordering the dinner, even figuring out which fork to use. If you keep practice dating, by the time you go out with Mr. or Ms. Wonderful, all that previously scary stuff will be second nature.

A CAUTION AND A GIFT

May I give you a caution and a gift? They are one and the same.

First, the caution: Don't "settle" out of comfort if you genuinely feel your practice date is not for you.

Now the gift: There is a chance that you will fall in love with one of your "stepping-stones." He or she could love you, appreciate you, make you feel good about yourself, and be a marvelous mate. Don't ignore this diamond in disguise. You might be much happier with this mate than if you stay on the lonely path of searching for the impossible dream.

Computer Dating: A Shy's Opportunity—or Trap?

We are fortunate to be living in this most exciting era. For example, it is spectacular that you can find like-minded people on the Internet. Sadly, for Shys, you seldom meet them face to face.

It is spectacular that you can telecommute to work. Sadly, for Shys, you don't get to chat around the watercooler.

It is spectacular that you can learn just about anything on the Internet. Sadly, for Shys, you don't use social skills while researching on the Web.

I am not in the least bit shy when I communicate with people by e-mail. I have been doing it for three years now and have communicated with lots of great guys. I can take all the time I want to get my thoughts together, correct them, and then reread it to make sure it sounds like what I genuinely mean to say. This helps someone to get to know the real me and I can get to know the real them.

—Sarah F., Northampton, Massachusetts

But can you, Sarah? When you're talking with someone face to face, you don't have the luxury to think five minutes before you respond. You can't push backspace/delete in a conversation. And personality and "chemistry" don't travel well in cyberspace.

Also consider that some of those "great guys" you're communicating with may be misrepresenting themselves. Is every tall, dark, handsome, brilliant, loving, caring, and honorable man who e-mails you really tall, dark, handsome, brilliant, loving, caring, and honorable?

I e-mailed Sarah to ask what some of these "great guys" were really like. She told me she hasn't had any face-to-face meetings yet. Hmm.

A WORD TO THE ROMANTICALLY SAVVY SHY

Many lifetime relationships started on a tiny computer screen. You know the sequence. Placing or answering an ad. Communicating by computer. Exchanging pictures. Having phone calls. Meeting. Dating. Mating. Marriage.

Sadly, Shys don't do well in the online love game. They often hide behind it and never meet their cyber pen pal. If they do and nothing clicks, they can plummet deeper into shyness. It can even shake the confidence of a Sure.

A good friend of mine, Ann, is good-looking, professional, smart, and a fabulous dresser—and she knows it. Because she hadn't yet found Mr. Right, she put an ad on a dating website and received several dozen responses. She wrote to six of them, had phone conversations with four, exchanged photos with three, and then agreed to meet two of them.

The first rendezvous point was a well-known restaurant. The meeting time was seven. She told her blind date that she'd be wearing a yellow pantsuit and a long orange scarf so there could be no way they'd miss.

Ann arrived on time and waited at the bar. She thought several men walking by looked like the photo she'd received, but she couldn't be sure.

By seven forty-five, she paid for her drink and left.

At eight, my phone rang. Ann's voice was bordering on the hysterical, "That's the first time in all my life that I've ever been stood up!"

Ann was usually pretty confident, but I knew that the experience had taken a big bite out of her ego when she said, "Leil, he must have been there, taken one look at me, and decided not to approach."

If that wasn't enough of a blow to her ego, she got clobbered by computer dating again. She met a doctor online and they made a date at a fine restaurant. Over cocktails, potential Dr. Right told her that an emergency had come up at the hospital and he wouldn't be able to stay for dinner.

"He apologized," Ann said, "and told me that my dinner check would be 'taken care of.' What an insult! Did he think I was some pauper? I know he was just buying me off because he didn't like me."

If Ann hadn't had a healthy self-image to start with, these experiences could have strangled her confidence forever.

Don't take a chance on your growing confidence being cut down before it fully blooms. Do more of the flirting and practice dating ShyBusters before you start exploring relationships in cyberspace.

ShyBuster #72
Computer Dating Is a Sure's Game

Proceed at your own risk with online dating. The first part of the trip is fun when you are still e-mailing your potential partner. But the road can take a dangerous turn when you meet. Your ego crashes if you are rejected.

When you become a Sure, the cheap shots will feel like a water gun on a duck's back and roll right off. For now, however, weigh the advantages and dangers carefully before you click "send." There will be plenty of time to enjoy these new twists on the old dating game when you've gotten your diploma from *Good-Bye to Shy*'s Stamping Out Shyness School.

Find People Who Share Your Passion

The old adage "Opposites attract" is true–but only for a short time. "Birds of a feather flock together" is the glue that holds most long-term relationships together.[51] All love seekers should scrounge the newspapers and surf the Web to find groups of people with the same interests. For Shy pursuers of love, it is almost essential. Just think of the benefits:

1. Approaching someone and making small talk is much easier when you share interests.
2. Making a date comes more naturally when an event of mutual interest comes up.
3. You don't suffer the stigma of being there for the obvious purpose of meeting someone. It's the mutual interest that draws you together.

EVEN MUSHROOMS SPROUT LOVE

I attended a faculty picnic after a college speech I gave a few years ago. After my talk, we sat on the campus lawn chatting and eating hamburgers. While talking with one of the teachers, 1 commented on a fortyish-looking man who had been sitting alone all afternoon.

"Oh, that's Professor Wagner," she said, "the head of the biology department. He's a very kind man. But he's shy and hardly talks to anyone. The only time he's comfortable is when he's in front of a class or talking about his field." She laughed. "Don't get him talking about mushrooms or he'll talk your ear off."

I wanted to meet this shy gentleman, so I crossed the park to introduce myself. From his demeanor, I could tell he was big-time shy.

I started the conversation, "Uh, Ms. Turner tells me you teach a course in mushrooms."

"Uh, yes," he said haltingly.

"I've always been interested in mushrooms," I lied. "Can you tell me a little about your class?"

He started slowly, but then, as the teacher had warned, the plug popped out of the dam. He started gushing about matsutakes, chanterelles, boletes, and a dozen names that I assume were mushrooms. My only contribution to his monologue was "How can you tell a poisonous one from a good one?"

That made it stunningly obvious that mushrooms weren't exactly my thing. He smiled and slithered back into his shy shell. After a rather lengthy moment of silence, he said, "You'll have to excuse me, I'm very shy." He then gave me one of the Shy's typical "Excuse me for taking up space on your planet" looks.

I told him that I was writing about the subject and asked if I could talk with him for a few minutes. He cautiously conceded but gave monosyllabic answers to most of my questions.

I guided the conversation to his private life. He told me that he was forty-two and that he would like to marry and maybe start a family, but he was too timid to ask any woman for a date. "And I don't meet many women. Besides," he added, "it's too late for me to think about getting married. All of the other professors already have children or teenagers."

"Professor Wagner," I asked, "are there any mushroom clubs? I mean, mushroom societies? I mean, associations? Well, groups of people of people who love mushrooms? Biologically, I mean. Not just for eating?"

Understandably, he looked at me confused. "Uh, I think so. But I wouldn't learn anything because, well, I probably know at least as much as they do about mushrooms."

He hadn't gotten the point. "Professor Wagner," I ventured, "may I make a suggestion?" He nodded. "I think you might enjoy going to a meeting of people who are interested in mushrooms. They would be very grateful if you shared your knowledge. You would be giving information instead of receiving. I highly suggest it."

Just then, we felt a drizzle from the sky, a sure sign that the picnic was over, and it was time to say our good-byes.

I felt sad that Professor Wagner hadn't picked up on my suggestion to attend some meetings or events where he could meet other people who shared his interests. Seizing on the example of the shy wine connoisseur from West Virginia who wrote me that she was able to make comfortable conversation at wine tastings, I had hoped Professor Wagner would enjoy socializing with some mushroom aficionados.

THE PROFESSOR'S SURPRISE

Several years passed, and the college invited me to speak there again. After my speech, I asked the event coordinator how Professor Wagner was doing and told her I'd like to say hello.

"Let me get his number for you." She looked at her faculty list. "I'm sure it will be OK if you call him at home."

I dialed his number, and a woman answered. Her voice was sweet but barely audible. I asked to speak to Professor Wagner. The next thing I heard was a soft, "Mike, honey, it's for you."

He seemed pleased that I'd called. Without sounding like I was trying to probe, I said, "The woman who answered has a lovely voice. Is she a relative?"

"Yes, she's my wife. And she is wonderful. Oh, I'm so sorry, Leil, I should have called you. After we spoke a few years ago, I thought about what you said and found a local league of mushroom lovers. I met Sandra there. It was a long time before either of us had the courage to approach the other. She's very shy but one time on a mushroom gathering trip, we started walking and talking together. We have so much in common. . . ."

Both Professor Wagner and Sandra are passionate about mushrooms. Happily, they now have each other to be passionate about, too.

ShyBuster #73
Meet Others Who Share Your Passion

Type the name of your hobby into an Internet search engine. Narrow the millions of hits by using the words *club*, *league*, *organization*, or *association* and further shave your choices by adding the name of your area. Chances are that you'll come up with a nearby group of people who are passionate about the same thing.

Find out what meetings or events the group has—and go! You never know who you might meet who shares your interests. To this day, I fantasize Professor Wagner and Sandra having a romantic tête-à-tête discussing spores—the sex life of fungi.

Two Sexy Little ShyBusters for "Almost Sures"

When you feel more relaxed giving a potential partner lingering looks (ShyBuster #70), here's an even sexier twist.

When two people are deeply in love, an interesting phenomenon occurs. While looking into each other's eyes, a dreaminess sets in. Even when they break eye contact, as they momentarily must, their eyes don't venture far from their partner.[52]

A ROMANTIC TACTIC FOR SHY MEN

If gazing into an attractive woman's eyes for an extended time is still difficult for you, use this "work-around." When you must break eye contact momentarily, do *not* look away from her. Especially don't look over her shoulder or appear to be looking elsewhere! You can briefly take your eyes off hers, but let them explore her face. It is especially pleasing to women when you have an expression of warmth and admiration when you do.

A SIZZLING TACTIC FOR SHY WOMEN

Shy women, you, too, can make your eye contact more sensuous. Very confident women have a naughty (but extremely effective) little trick. When taking their eye contact break, they sometimes take it on his chest. They gaze at his body and then look into his eyes and give him an approving little smile.

Shy ladies, when you are feeling a bit more confident, you can do a more subtle version of that. While he is speaking to you, take just a flickering glance at his chest. Follow this with a little smile to let him know you liked what you saw. In this case, your smile can even be a shy one because that expresses that you're feeling a tad "guilty" for what you've done. You will see his immediate positive reaction as he puffs up the chest that you have just silently admired.

ShyBuster #75
Women, Let Your Eyes Wander a Little Farther

Women, you have an invitation to let your eyes travel a little farther south on his body. During eye contact breaks, take a fleeting visit to his chest. Then smilingly return your eyes to his. He will thoroughly enjoy your little voyage.

Needless to say, men, do *not* use this ShyBuster on women. The neck is as far south as you dare go without her considering you lecherous.

Enticing Attire for Shys

Now let's talk about your "hunting gear" for finding a special someone. No way is it "unisex" clothing!

Women, because you like a man dressed in good quality clothes, you might think he'll admire your new designer pantsuit. Probably not. A man is more attracted by a sexy outfit.

Men, because you like sexy clothes on women, you may think she'll be turned on by your sleeveless shirt and tight jeans. Probably not. Most women prefer quality material, color coordination, and a good fit.

This is not just speculation. A study published in the *Archives of Sexual Behavior* proved that the particular clothes a woman wore were practically meaningless to a man as long as she looked desirable. Conversely, women were much more attracted to men who wore high-quality, coordinated clothes.[53]

I hope that by now you have both packed away your dreary clothing and are donning more attention-getting and attractive clothing every day. (If not, go back to ShyBuster #35, "Chuck the Dull Duds." When you get into the more conspicuous clothing habit, come back here and continue "dressing for finding love.")

THIS TIME, LADIES FIRST

Women, most men can't tell your top designer gown from a Target fire sale–and they could care less. But instinctively and instantaneously they spot skin–a little cleavage here, a little more leg there.

Naturally, you don't want to look like a lady of the night, so you must plan some very subtle sexy revelations. Wear, say, a conservative jacket but with a scanty blouse underneath. When the jacket "accidentally" comes unbuttoned across the room or across the table, it "accidentally" reveals, ahem, a couple of your assets.

Ditto with an appropriate-length skirt. No one can blame you if it happens to ride up a tad higher on your legs when you spot a nice gentleman.

Please don't misunderstand me. I'm not suggesting that you do anything shameless, just a little tantalizing.

At first, drawing this type of attention to yourself may be agonizing. But it has manifold benefits. It's not only for enticing men. It helps you gain more appreciation of your own body.

ShyBuster #76
Women, Dress a Little Daring

One of the most difficult challenges for a shy woman is to draw attention to herself. But look at it this way. If you work out, you wear sweatpants. If you play tennis, you wear a tennis skirt. If you ride horses, you wear jodhpurs. And, if you're looking for love, you wear something ever so slightly suggestive. Never compromise your principles, of course, but do dress a little more sensuously at appropriate times.

GUYS, REVEALING CLOTHES FOR YOU?

Generally, no. You might think a woman is attracted by your revealing clothes. Not usually. Pack away those sleeveless shirts and bun-hugging jeans when you're looking for love.

A woman is very particular when it comes to your clothing. My seminar participants are always surprised when I tell them that studies prove that the clothes a man wears are more important to a woman than vice versa.[54]

"Why," you might ask, "does a woman care so much about what I'm wearing?" Because, gentlemen, it is in her genes.

"Her what?"

Her genes—meaning that instinctively she wants to know that you could take care of her and her unborn children. It is subconscious, of course, but coordinated clothes show that you are discerning and careful. Quality fabrics reveal that you probably have the means to do so.

ShyBuster #77
Men, Go for Quality and Coordination

Go for quality, not quantity in clothing. Because women usually have a better instinct for clothing, recruit your sister to go shopping with you—or even your mom.

Buy a few top-quality shirts, slacks, and shoes. If your lifestyle requires that you wear a suit, break the bank for just one good one that will last forever. Don't forget to coordinate your colors—no black pants with brown belts or shoes. And get long socks, not the ones that (horror of horrors) show a little hairy leg.

(57)

Don't Mistake Sex for Love

O n another trip to my hometown, I ran into Lynda, a girl who lived across the street from me when I was in high school. We had a great time laughing about all of the neighborhood "characters" we'd known and the same kids we'd babysat. Lynda had a sister, Carrina, who was extremely good-looking. When I was in high school, I'd often hear her coming home from a date in the wee hours in the morning. I asked Lynda, "How is Carrina? Does she still live in Bethesda?"

Lynda's face fell. "Nearby," she answered, mentioning a downtrodden part of Washington, D.C.

Seeing Lynda's dismay, I thought it prudent to change the subject, "How about your mom. She's doing well?"

"Oh she's great, but . . . Carrina has her problems." I was silent, realizing that Lynda did indeed want to talk about her sister.

She showed me a photo from her wallet of Carrina, a man, and three kids. "Carrina's living with another guy now." I couldn't believe it was the same girl. She looked haggard and almost older than Lynda's age and mine put together.

"Uh, cute kids," was the only thing I could think of to say.

"All different dads. I know what you're thinking, Leil."

I was. "What happened?"

"Carrina was a bright girl and she had terrific looks going for her."

"She really did. I saw how popular she was. Lots of dates."

"Too many. But that was because she 'put out' for any guy who dated her, even once." Lynda gave a wry smile. "I guess she was just the gal who couldn't say no."

OVERSEXED OR UNDERCONFIDENT?

"I don't understand," I said. "Was she oversexed?"

"No, underconfident. Still is. In fact, she told me that she didn't even enjoy the sex part, but she was so shy she didn't want to say 'no' to any guy. She was afraid he'd give her a hassle. So she'd just go along with anything the guy wanted.

"I think she felt worthless and figured she could never get love in any other way. She mistook sex for affection."

Healthy love usually culminates in sex. But don't let loneliness convince you that it works the other way, too. Everyone should think carefully before deciding to have sex—especially Shys.

ShyBuster #78
Don't Get Caught in the "Sex Love Trap"

Shys, you are more sensitive than most people. And, therefore, more vulnerable and more easily hurt. Sex is a big step, and the last thing you need right now is heartbreak. Look before you leap into bed with someone.

How do you tell whether someone is right for you? It's a complicated and often long process. It begins with getting to know the other person well—and letting them get to know you. Be sure they like and respect you before taking the next step.

Shy men, this goes for you, too. Only you can judge, of course, but, because you are more sensitive to feelings, consider holding off on sex until it feels right for both of you.

SHY BABY SISTER OR CLASS SLUT?

Lynda looked at the photo of her sister sadly. "She got known as the 'school slut.' None of the girls wanted to be seen with her, and neither did the guys. Oh, they wanted to screw her at night, all right. But not talk to her at school. Pretty soon it got to the point where they'd pick her up, take her to their place, do it, and bring her back afterward. Sometimes they'd even send her back on the bus.

"And she was such a sweet kid . . ."

PART

11

For Parents and Shys Who Want to Know Why (and How to Prevent It!)

Why me? Why am I shy? Was I born this way? Who caused this? Mom and Dad? Those bullies who lived down the block? My teachers? My great-grandmother on my father's side? Or did God say, "Somebody's got to be shy"–and I got chosen?

It could be any of these (except the last, of course). Read on to explore the reasons why you in particular might be shy–and some things you can do to rewrite your history. If you're a parent, I've included tips on how to determine your baby's risk for shyness–and how to help your shy child.

— • —

Born Shy?

Some people are, indeed, "born shy." Or, at least, they are at higher risk of becoming shy. But genes are not destiny. Nor is there actually a "shy gene." Scientists didn't look into the microscope and say, "Ah ha, there's the little bugger, the shy gene." However, 20 to 30 percent of babies are born with a brain chemistry that makes them more apt to become shy.[55]

Parents, if your child was one of the sensitive babies who is more prone to shyness, it would have shown up early. Just one month after carrying your little bundle of joy home, you could have determined whether he or she were the type of newborn that the shyness bug likes to feast on.

DETERMINING IF YOU OR YOUR CHILD IS A "BORN SHY"

A landmark study proved that some newborns have a higher proclivity toward shyness. Two of the world's top shyness researchers brought 400 one-month-old infants into their laboratory.[56] They put a creepy toy in the infants' cribs, gave each a whiff of alcohol on a Q-tip, and played a recording of a stranger's voice for them.

Almost a third of the babies freaked out, howling and flailing their tiny arms and legs. After their traumatic incident, they clung tightly to a parent. Years later, the researchers discovered that those particular babies suffered shyness. We will call this type of Shy a "Highly Sensitive Shy," or "HSS."

In contrast, approximately two-thirds of the infants took the obnoxious intrusions in their stride. They simply shoved the ghastly toy and stinky stuff away and then smiled at the stranger's voice.

The researchers' hypothesis was proven.

Approximately one-third of babies' body chemistry makes them extra sensitive to unfamiliar events and people, and therefore more susceptible to becoming shy.[57]

–SCIENCE

GIVE OR TAKE THE "CRIB TEST"

Parents of newborns, you can replicate this research to discover your baby's proclivity for shyness.

Your research instruments? One: A weird toy–maybe a creepy black rubber spider. Two: Something stinky. (No, not her own full diapers. That is an everyday fragrance for her.) Three: the postman, a next door neighbor, or anyone else your baby has never seen.

First step: Dangle the hideous toy above her crib. *Watch her reaction.*

Second step: Wave the stinky stuff under her tiny nose. *Watch her reaction.*

Third step: Tell the stranger to say "koochie koochie koo." *Watch her reaction.*

Sensitive babies will react more frantically to these new stimuli, whereas those who are not prone to shyness will just say "yuuuck" in baby talk and push it away.

As a baby, our daughter was so sensitive she couldn't stand being held by anybody but Mommy and Daddy (and sometimes even Daddy was not on her accepted list). It was a very trying time. She may have been colicky to start, but, as she grew older as a preschooler, this sensitivity grew into what many might call "shy," characterized by avoiding people's eyes when she first met them, not talking to them, and hanging behind Mom's and Dad's legs rather than socializing with people.

–Steve C., Vancouver, British Columbia[58]

ShyBuster #79
Give Your Infant the "Crib Test"

Parents: To determine whether your new baby is prone to shyness, observe his or her crib behavior. If your baby reacts strongly to new stimuli, he may become shy. (However, you can do the ShyBusters in this section to help circumvent it.) Does your baby take it all in stride? Then she was probably not born shy.

Shys: To help determine whether you were a sensitive baby with a tendency toward shyness, ask your parents or guardians how you reacted to new stimuli when you were a little crib crawler.

Four Years Later

For the relentless researchers, the experiment was far from over. Four years after their first observation, they brought the 400 little subjects back into the lab. Sure enough, most of the tots who had tested highly sensitive showed incipient signs of shyness.

About half those highly sensitive babies grew into being extremely timid teens.

My daughter is what her psychologist calls "slow-to-warm." She comes off shy until she knows someone, but eventually she settles in and opens up, so people think she is just shy. It actually runs much deeper. It has to do with everything in her life. If she isn't familiar with a situation, she has a significant amount of anxiety, even over the littlest of things. For example, she's in fourth grade and her class was taking a field trip to the state capitol. She's been in this school with these kids since kindergarten and has even shown her horse in Lansing a number of times. But she had never been to the state capitol and didn't know what to expect. The night before the trip, she couldn't sleep, was nauseous, and so on.

–Steve C., Vancouver, British Columbia

A NATURAL INTROVERT OR "HIGHLY SENSITIVE SHY"?

Unfortunately, HSSs often assume that something is wrong with them because they're not "look at me" types. If you are a highly sensitive person, your brain functions differently from an extrovert's. You think more deeply. It takes you longer to process information. You try to listen carefully and usually speak more slowly.

Americans listen to outrageous radio and television personalities. We elect outgoing politicians. We listen to extreme rock bands, adore scantily clad show-off girls, and flock in droves to theaters to see bigger-than-life movie stars–and then stay up half the night to see them again on the Oscars.

Regrettably, our Western world does not recognize or reward introvert qualities as much as it does extrovert. As a result, some HSSs assume they are not as smart or as talented as the Sures.

Stop! Wrong way! Go back! Countless studies have blasted the myth about shyness indicating stupidity. In many cases, in fact, it's just the opposite.

The majority of gifted children (60 percent) are introverts. In studies of intelligence, the higher the IQ, the higher the percentage of introverts. A greater number of National Merit Scholars are introverted than extroverted, and they get higher grades in Ivy League colleges.[59]

What this says is this: Value your God-given qualities and don't let anyone make you feel inferior because you don't like to sit around with the gang and chew the fat or to leap into conversations before you've thought things through. Even extremely confident, highly sensitive people take longer to process their thoughts. Give deserved worth to your inner world and become comfortable with your quieter qualities.

A CONFIDENT INTROVERT

Recently, an extremely successful yet soft-spoken woman named Cheryl engaged me to do a speech in Phoenix, Arizona. While driving to the convention hall, I told her that I was writing a book on shyness. A few weeks later, I received this surprise e-mail from her.

Leil, our conversation struck a familiar chord with me. I have struggled with "shyness" all of my life, feeling like I'm marching to a different drummer than most of the world. I couldn't understand why many of my schoolmates and coworkers enjoyed talking with lots of people and spending large amounts of time visiting. I preferred just one or two close friends, more intimate settings, and deeper conversation. I couldn't figure out why I would rather remain in the background and think about a topic before speaking, while others would vocalize their thoughts without restraint. I couldn't fathom how people who became my closest and dearest friends would later tell me that they thought I was "cold" or "aloof" upon first impression—but realized I was "anything but" after they got to know me. I was very intelligent, always an honors student, and later an excellent businessperson. I truly liked people. But I couldn't seem to get the hang of the whole socializing bit. I wondered if something was "wrong" with me.

—Cheryl M., Phoenix, Arizona

Cheryl's poignant message continues with her self-discovery and her conclusions. It finishes with how she now leads a successful and joyful life within the framework of her more sensitive nature. Due to its length, you will find Cheryl's full letter in Appendix A.

As you go about your daily life, remember that HSSs are usually people of high integrity and compassion. They are not often conspicuous leaders of crowds, but they are leaders by example: thinkers, advisors, healers. They are very fair and have many other qualities that have a positive effect on society.[60]

Inherited Shyness?

MOM'S EYES AND DAD'S SHYNESS

Can you inherit shyness? That's like asking whether you can inherit long legs or brown eyes. Sure you can. But it's not a rule. For instance, I have a girlfriend who groans, "My brother inherited Mom's long black eyelashes, and I got Dad's stubby pale ones." Not fair, but there's nothing she can do about it. Genes will go where they want.

It's the same with inheriting shyness. It's a roll of the dice. Nevertheless, a study called "Childhood Shyness and Maternal Social Phobia" found that children who had shy mothers are eight times more likely to be shy themselves. Twenty percent of Shys have first-degree relatives with a phobia.[61]

By unearthing the origins of your shyness, you can achieve more realistic goals. For example, people who inherited their shyness usually have an extra-sensitive nature, and they should not struggle to become extroverts. Research shows that only extremely rarely will they succeed. More important, these sensitive people would not be happy as extroverts.

ShyBuster #80
Shake Your Family Tree for Shyness

Parents: Are you or have you ever been shy? If so, perhaps there is a genetic link to your child's shyness. What about other relatives? Were your parents shy? (Some qualities skip a generation and then reappear.) If you answered "yes" to either of these questions, take extra care to curb your child's shyness.

Shys: Dig through your genealogy with a fine-tooth hacksaw. Are there any suspects? If so, knowing it gives you some perspective that will help you fight your shyness.

(60)

Are You a Closet Extrovert or "Situational Shy"?

Suppose you were a blasé baby who wasn't the least bit fazed by scary toys and stinky stuff in the crib. Nor could you shake any Shys out of your family tree. It could indicate that experiences while growing up probably affected your personality. You could be called a "Situational Shy," or "SS."

IS SHYNESS A COMMUNICABLE DISEASE?

You can't "catch" a case of shyness. If your guardians were shy, however, even if they weren't your parents, there is a greater chance you will be, too. We tend to imitate people we are around, especially parental types.

A child hardly ever recognizes that a parent is shy.[62] It's only these many years later, for example, that I realize that my mother was. One Thanksgiving when I was about fourteen, we visited a slew of relatives we hadn't seen in a long time. Aunt Lucy was jabbering away. Uncle Charley had a turkey hat on his head–and I suspect a few drinks under his belt. My other relatives were chattering simultaneously. And there was Mama, sitting as quiet as a clam, hands folded. And I, like a little clamlet, sat silently beside her.

I admired my mother so much that had she jumped on Aunt Lucy's new dining room table and danced an Irish jig, I'd be right along aside her kicking up my heels. But Mama hardly ever spoke up in a group. So I didn't, either.

We never had any friends because we lived out in the country on a farm and there weren't many other kids who were my age around. The mothers of the other kids arranged a lot of times when they all got together to play. But my mother never did. When I got older, my dad told me she was shy. Looking back, I wonder if the reason I didn't have many friends was because she was too shy and wonder if that's the reason she didn't call the other parents.

–Ariana G., Taos, New Mexico

Think way back to your toddlerhood. Did Mommy and Daddy socialize very much? Did they often have friends visit them? Did they belong to any clubs or go to meetings? Did they talk on the phone a lot? Did they ever give parties? Did they encourage or arrange ways for you to play with the other kids? If not, you may have found the key to your shyness.

ShyBuster #81
Beware "Mommy See, Mommy Do"

Parents: Remember that you are a role model for your kids. If you are shy, make an extra effort to whoop it up a bit in front of your progeny. They will enjoy seeing you have fun and will follow your lead. Reach out to other parents to arrange outings and playdates. Your kids will thank you.

Shys: Remind yourself that, as a kid, you were simply acting as you thought you should. Recognizing that you were simply copying family members can give you the confidence you need to break the pattern. Situational Shys, try to recall all of the situations when your parents showed timid behavior. Then visualize yourself handling that same situation with more courage and confidence.

Bullies in Bygone Days?

A RASPBERRY TO REMEMBER

Every Shy (or ex-Shy) cringes when remembering an excruciatingly humiliating moment. I even shudder now as I write about one of mine.

In third grade, the most difficult part of my school day was math class. Not because the numbers were mind-boggling. Not because I hated my math teacher. But because of my acute shy attacks.

The math teacher often gave us an exercise and then left the room for a few minutes. With furrowed brows, the other girls would finish the exercise, then they would start clucking like a bunch of baby chickens until the teacher returned. But I, the shy ostrich, buried my head in my books and pretended to still be working.

One unforgettable day, the teacher gave us an exercise and then, as usual, left the room. During those silent working minutes, I felt the urgent need to pass gas (commonly known then as a "raspberry"). As the gas flooded through me, I knew I would be unable to halt its escape. Thanks to our Maker, I managed to let the air out silently and slowly. It sailed away, and, with a sigh of relief, I went back to tackling my math assignment.

Less than thirty seconds later, one of the girls, Sonia, lifted her head and said, "I smell raspberries." Laughter from all.

"I wonder where it's coming from," another girl chirped. More uproarious laughter.

"Let's find out!" Sonia pronounced with the determination of Sherlock Holmes. Then the nightmare began. Like an Easter egg hunt, Sonia began the festive search for the origins of the scent.

Starting at the other side of the room, she crawled up and down each row dramatically sniffing everybody—much to the hilarity of all of the confident girls who knew they were not culpable.

When she got to my row, I became hysterical. I grabbed my books and bolted out, tears streaming down my face. As I raced down the hall, I heard a cruel chorus behind me chanting, "It was Leilie. It was Leilie. It was Leilie."

Fifty-eight percent of Shys can recall a traumatic social experience near the onset of their symptoms. Forty-four percent remember one intense episode, which they felt started it.[63]

–JOURNAL OF ABNORMAL PSYCHOLOGY

Before I started school, therefore before I was even five years old, I had to go to the hospital for what probably was only three or four days, but my memory is that it was an eternity. I was in a children's ward. I had the bed in the corner. I was the only boy in the ward—all the others were girls. But I would have been too young to understand gender difference. I would not talk to anyone. Some of the other children were quite loud and extraverted, they clowned around a lot. Particularly the girl in the bed in the opposite corner. I often cried. She would be the one to notice and loudly make fun of it to all the others. I would roll over facedown and pretend to be asleep.

I was too shy to ask where the toilets were, so at least daily I would wet the bed. The nurses got increasingly angry that I kept doing this and yelled at me in front of the girls.

–Nathan F., Green Bay, Wisconsin

IT'S THE BULLIES, NOT YOU

Most little kids don't mean to be cruel. Without thinking, however, they can be vicious. The *Journal of Clinical Child Psychology* cites a study called "Predictors of Peer Rejection in Early Elementary Grades" that confirms the harmful effects of these early episodes.[64]

One single experience doesn't make a kid shy if she is not sensitive to start with. But it sure doesn't help! Even if a Shy doesn't have one early horror story to point to, how well she feels accepted in school is crucial.[65] It becomes a template of her expectations in later years.

Parents, it's important to look for signs that your child is being bullied. Signals include torn clothes, missing belongings, unexplained injuries, fear of walking to the school bus, taking an unusual route to school, and so on. If you see any of these signs, talk to your child about it and convince him that it's the bullies' fault–not his. Don't tell him to physically fight them. Do, however, encourage him to face bullies with a strong erect "Stop it!" instead of cowering. You can even rehearse this with your child.

If the bullying behavior continues, talk to your child's teacher about it.

ShyBuster #82
Replay the Early Show

Parents: If you suspect that your child is being bullied, you need to take steps to assure your child's confidence isn't damaged. You must become (1) a detective (analyze the situation); (2) a psychologist (ask questions and talk with your child about it); (3) an advisor (suggest ways to respond); and (4) a theatrical director (do some role-playing). If nothing changes, you must become (5) a teacher's confidante (talk with the teacher). Sometimes it's appropriate to talk with the bully's parents too, and let them know what their child is up to.

Shys: Thoughtless youngsters can really mess up a sensitive little kid's head. If you're one of the 58 percent of Shys who can remember one specific childhood experience, run it through your mind. Inevitably, you will come to the conclusion that it was the other kid's cruelty, not your conduct, that was at fault. Contemplate it until you are convinced. Then revisualize the situation and see yourself handling the situation with the knowledge you have today.

Mom's and Dad's Overprotection?

DAHLING, MY SHRINK SAID . . .

Forty years ago in America, it was chic to have a psychiatrist. Anybody who was anybody (or who thought they were) decorated their conversation with, "Well, my shrink said . . ."

They often ended complaints with, "It was all my parents' fault."

Whether or not psychologists actually did accuse parents, that was the common cop-out for any shortcomings. (And people paid a lot of time and money for this excuse.)

But was it really your parents' "fault" that you became shy? Again, the revered and reliable researchers who have dedicated their lives to explore the roots and results of shyness came up with the right answer: "For some it was, for some it wasn't."

Children who have been overprotected by their parents do, however, run a much higher risk of being shy. A study called "The Development of Anxiety: The Role of Control in the Early Environment" found that:

> Parents who exert maximal control over a child's activities and decisions can negatively influence the child's sense of being able to control his or her own environment.[66]
>
> −PSYCHOLOGY BULLETIN

I wish two of two of my longtime friends had known this. Steve and Lydia are a wonderful couple who have only one son. After he was born, Lydia wasn't able to have more children, so little Lenny became obsessively precious to them. If three-month-old Lenny started crying while I was visiting, Lydia would hop to her feet before my next sentence and sprint to the nursery. Sounds of her baby talk wafted into the living room. "Ooh, did some big black bear come to bite my widddle baby? Awww, Mommy's here now. Everything is going to be all wight."

Frankly, I found it nauseating. That doesn't mean that if I had a kid, I'd lock him in the nursery and let him scream like a sick coyote. But I certainly wouldn't come running every time he hiccoughed.

We had dinner together at a restaurant several times when Lenny was not so "widdle" any more, about eight years old. Unfortunately, adult conversation was futile. Whenever the little prince burped, there was an anxious duet of "Oh, Lenny. Are you OK?" "Did the nasty Coca Cola make you burp?"

One night Lydia told him, "We'll order you an orange juice."

Lenny crossed his arms and announced, "I hate orange juice. I hate orange juice. I hate orange juice."

I was about to gag. "Don't you think Lenny would enjoy eating at home next time?" I asked. "I know a wonderful babysitter who cooks, too. My treat."

"I hate babysitters!" whined the little bugger. (Can you sense I was getting a tad emotional about this?)

Lydia leaned over and whispered, "Lenny doesn't like babysitters."

"I sort of picked that up," I said.

"What other drinks can I have?" Lenny interrupted.

This was war. I looked right at him and said, "Lenny, why don't *you* ask the waitress?"

Lydia and Steve just laughed and called the waitress over. Lenny looked at his mother and loudly declared, "I want a root beer." Lydia then turned to the waitress. "He'd like a root beer."

"The waitress isn't hard of hearing," I mumbled.

Where's Lenny Now?

I didn't see my friends for ten years because they moved to Michigan. But recently I was giving a speech in Detroit and called them. When they arrived at the restaurant, for the first time, there was no Lenny!

When I asked about him, Steve and Lydia looked at each other painfully. Lydia said, "He didn't want to come."

Hallelujah! "Oh, that's too bad," I said.

Steve and Lydia spent the next hour lamenting that he was "uncomfortable around people." He had no friends. He wouldn't go to parties. At eighteen, he'd never had a date. He was shy and felt the other kids didn't like him. "So we home-schooled him."

I had to bite my tongue. It was obvious. By doing everything for Lenny and indulging his every whim, he never developed the social skills or the courage to do things on his own.

GO PLAY IN THE TRAFFIC

Obviously, parents, you aren't going to tell your kids that. Do, however, progressively give them increasingly more complicated challenges. Suppose that you and your six-year-old daughter are at a restaurant, and she is served a baked potato with sour cream and butter on it. But little Petunia doesn't like sour cream on her potato.

She complains, "Mommy, I want just butter. Tell her to take it back." Mom, your ideal response would be, "Petunia, why don't you tell her yourself? I'll call her over for you, but you must ask her to take the sour cream away." Little by little, give your kids increasingly bigger challenges appropriate to their age.

My mother and I were very close, maybe because my father died when I was two and I am an only child. I don't know when it began, but by the time I got to grade school, I realized that my mother was much more protective of me than the other kids' mothers. I wasn't even allowed to cross the street alone to play with the other kids. It didn't bother me that much because she would take me to the movies a lot and we would go away together on every vacation. I liked that because I didn't have to be around other kids who would tease me. I think they thought I was a snob because I didn't play with them.

I was so shy in high school, especially around boys, that my mother put me in a small private tutoring school where we had only five or six people to a class. I'm thirty-four now and still live with my mother. I've hardly ever dated because I get so nervous around men that the few times I have been asked out, I've said no. I realize I have to change but it's hard to break old patterns and thought habits.

–Linda G., Carrollton, Ohio

DADS, A BETTER INFLUENCE?

Congratulations, Dads. Yes, generally you are actually a better influence on your child's shyness than your wife. Why? Because if another kid bullies your son and comes home with a scratched knee, you are more apt to say, "Get out there, kid, and tell him he can't treat you like that." Mommy is more likely to croon sympathetically and kiss the booboo.

In one study, fathers were so brusque in pushing their kids to stick up for themselves that even the researchers were shocked. But they had to admit, it worked.

By pushing the child to change, thus appearing insensitive and intrusive, fathers may have influenced their sons to become less inhibited.[67]

–*JOURNAL OF DEVELOPMENTAL PSYCHOPATHOLOGY*

That definitely does not mean to ignore them. Parents who have a strong bond with their children (including love, open communication, dependability) and exert low control (in other words, encouraging them to do things on their own) are the most likely to have confident children.

ShyBuster #83
Don't Baby Your Baby

Parents: Moms and Dads, of course you love your kids—but do *not* do everything for them. Let them know that they can depend on you. Then progressively encourage them to do more and more on their own. If your children need encouragement and practice, try doing some role-playing to help them work through various situations.

Shys: You know how painful shyness is and you now have more information than your parents did on how to prevent it. So, if you have, or plan to have, kids of your own, don't baby *your* babies.

Getting to Know Yourself and Love Yourself and Becoming a "Certified Sure"

Many people, if asked the question, "Who are you?" might answer, "I'm a mother," "I'm a Mexican," "I'm a magician," "I'm a Muslim," and so on.

Whoa! Stop! Go back! You are so much more than your role in life, your nationality, your job, or your religion. You are a multifaceted mixture of an immeasurable number of thoughts, feelings, qualities—all unique. Discovering precisely who you are and what you want from life is a secret to lifetime confidence. That's the ultimate step in saying "good-bye to shy" forever.

We'll do that here, and then you'll design a graduation party for yourself.

Five Minutes a Day for a Priceless Gift

In the 1960s, technology empowered us to travel to outer space. Now technology allows us to travel in the other direction, to inner space. Thanks to neuroimaging, hardly a week goes by when scientists don't discover unknown regions of the brain that hold mysterious memories and incredible emotional experiences.

You probably don't want to shave your head, go to a lab, and wire your brain for magnetic resonance imaging to see why you act the way you do. But you can do the next best thing. A potent weapon to battle shyness is deep knowledge of yourself. It is not a long or strenuous trip. It is surprisingly easy for the value you receive.

Sadly, even though Shys concentrate on themselves, few of them develop a solid sense of identity. Most Shys really don't know themselves. And how can you love someone you don't understand?

> Many social phobics never feel complete. They never attain a satisfactory "sense of self."[68]
>
> —*COMMUNICATION EDUCATION*

LOOK HOW FAR YOU'VE ALREADY COME IN SELF-KNOWLEDGE

You have already started the quest because . . .

- You know what gives you the jitters (ShyBuster #16), and you have categorized them from least to most intimidating (ShyBuster #17).
- You have learned that, when it comes to social situations, you perform better than you think you do (ShyBuster #14).
- You now know that people regard you more highly than you believe (ShyBuster #9).
- You have thought seriously about your job (ShyBuster #36).
- You have gotten familiar with your facial expressions and smile (ShyBuster #27).
- You have realized how much your body language conveys, too (ShyBuster #44).
- You have contemplated how you felt about the most common topics of conversation (ShyBuster #54).
- You then listed the topics that you are extremely knowledgeable about (ShyBuster #55).
- Finally, you asked yourself some serious questions, "What are my passions?" "What do I feel deeply enough to spend my valuable time working toward that cause?" (ShyBuster #58)

Now is the time to begin the most significant self-knowledge search of all. It is one that I created during a frightening part of my life. I credit ShyBuster #84 for bringing me back to the security and joy that I now feel every day.

"SELF, WHAT DO YOU THINK ABOUT . . ."

Self-knowledge is knowing how you, personally, feel about a wide range of profound issues.

Choose a quiet time each day, perhaps while shaving, putting on makeup, or traveling to work. Or even just before going to bed. Ask yourself questions as though you were a radio host interviewing yourself. Answer one soul-searching question each day. Ponder it thoroughly. Even if you have a quick answer, continue focusing on that concept for the full five minutes so that it will be deeply embedded in your psyche.

Some sample questions could be:

Do I have a purpose on earth? If so, what is it?
Who is the God of my understanding?
What do honor, success, family, and friendship mean to me?

Your self-interview might go something like this:
Self, if you had a lot of money to donate to a charity, which one would it be?

"Well, you know, Self, I've never really thought about it. But every time I see blind people, my heart goes out to them. I always wish I could give them their sight back, but, of course, that's not within my power. I guess I'd donate to help research on blindness or to a school for the blind."

That's wonderful, Self.

"Well, thanks, Self. But, hey, that's just me."

You'll find 100 self-knowledge questions in Appendix B. They can comprise your first months of self-exploration.

ShyBuster #84
Travel to Inner Space

Be a radio or television host and interview yourself for a full five minutes each day. Thoroughly answer just one of the self-knowledge questions in Appendix B. You will be thrilled how quickly you cultivate a significant sense of who you are and how you feel. As you listen to your own answers, you'll also realize that you are a pretty admirable person. This knowledge will add immeasurably to your confidence.

In addition to giving yourself one of the greatest gifts of a lifetime, the strong sense of your own self, you will never again hesitate when meaningful subjects come up in conversation. You won't need the extra time to formulate your ideas because you've already done that. You can answer questions quickly and give your opinion confidently.

The self-knowledge questions at the back of the book are just for starters. When you finish them, write and answer more. When you finish these, write questions that relate personally to your life and the people you know. For example, you might ask yourself, "How do I really feel about my loudmouthed brother-in-law?"–and realize that he's a pretty good egg after all.

(64)

Graduation Day

Let me tell you about the night I knew that I was "cured." Daffy and I were working a trip to London and, while chatting in the galley, Daf told me she was proud of me.

"Why?" I smiled. But I knew why. It was because now I was comfortably looking right into my passengers' eyes whenever I asked, "Would you like coffee? Or perhaps you would prefer tea?" (Flight attendants spoke in complete sentences in those days.)

I already felt like a successful student. But, on our London layover, she gave me another of those now-familiar "I've-got-something-up-my-sleeve" expressions.

"Uh oh," I said. But this time I didn't mind, because her help with my self-styled Graduated Exposure Therapy had worked wonders. She whispered, "We're going someplace tonight, and you are going to be just as friendly to the people there as you were to my mother's Greek friends."

I was feeling pretty cocky about my progress. "Sure, Daf, anywhere you want."

After we'd slept off the jet lag, done a little shopping, and had a bite to eat, we hopped on one of those wonderful old red double-deckered London buses. Daffy still hadn't told me where she was taking me. At each stop, I'd press my nose against the window and ask, "Here?"

"Nope."

"Here?"

"Nope."

The next stop was in front of the Playboy Club on Park Lane. "Here?" I joked.

"Yes!"

I held on to my seat. "Oh no, Daffy. You're not getting me in there."

She yanked me up. "Oh yes, I am."

"Do they allow women without bunny tails in?" I mumbled as she dragged me to the door.

As the maitre'd wound his way through the crowd taking us to our table, I noticed a number of men momentarily ungluing their eyes from the bunnies' fluffy tails and silk ears to look at us. Emboldened by the confidence I'd felt in the Greek restaurant, I stood up straight, brushed my hair back, and even smiled at a few of them.

FROM SCARED RABBIT TO BOLD BUNNY

One of the Playboy bunnies must have noticed my excitement. While doing the graceful "bunny dip" serving our drinks, she whispered to me, "I have an extra pair of bunny ears in the back if you'd like to wear them."

Daffy gasped when I gleefully placed them on my head. "Hey, cool it," she said. "Now you're going too far!"

I really was, and it was thrilling. I had gone from a scared, masked rabbit timidly taking kids trick-or-treating to a blatant bunny showing off in the Playboy Club. I wanted to dance and shout, "I'm free–I'm no longer shy!"

At that moment, I started planning a little surprise party for Daffy's birthday. Me, a party giver? *That* was the confirmation that I'd won the battle!

Meanwhile, throughout the evening, several men came to our table to chat. While they were ordering drinks for us, Daffy leaned over and whispered, "Go, girl. Nobody would ever guess you were shy."

I winked at her, "I'll just keep faking it 'til I make it." But I wasn't faking it anymore.

IT'S TIME FOR THE BIG TEST

Think of it as the SATs, the bar exam, or a board certification. There are exams to become an R.N., CPA, Ph.D., even a GHRS (Ghosts and Hauntings Researcher). So why not an exam to prove you are no longer a Shy? You are now a certified "Sure." There are two parts: (1) show off by doing something silly and (2) then give yourself a Graduation Party.

ShyBuster #85
Take the "Confidence Certification" Exam

When you've finished all the ShyBusters, celebrate by showing off. Let your imagination go wild. Do something safe but silly to show you've gone from Shy to Screwy—like most happy "Super Sures" are.

Then plan an office birthday celebration for a colleague. Or invite the boys to your place for a Super Bowl bash. Nobody will know, as you lift your glass, that you're really toasting your own Success over Shyness. It's proof you graduated from a Party Panicker to Party Planner, from Shy to Confident.

If you don't succeed at first, don't be disheartened. Simply go back and repeat some of the ShyBusters. Soon, you, too, will be wearing your graduation cap, although probably not silk bunny ears. Choose a baseball cap, beret, helmet, turban, tiara, or just an invisible crown. You will silently and ecstatically shout, *I'm free! I'm no longer shy!* Nobody will hear you, of course, just your new confident self. And that's the most important person in the world.

Appendix A
Cheryl's Full Letter

Dear Leil,

I have struggled with "shyness" all of my life, feeling like I'm marching to a different drummer than most of the world. I couldn't understand why many of my schoolmates and coworkers enjoyed talking with lots of people and spending large amounts of time visiting when I preferred just one or two close friends, more intimate settings, and deeper conversation. I couldn't figure out why I would rather remain in the background and think about a topic before speaking, while others would vocalize their thoughts without restraint. I couldn't fathom how people who became my closest and dearest friends would later tell me that they thought I was "cold" or "aloof" upon first impression but realized I was "anything but" after they got to know me. I was very intelligent, always an honors student, and later an excellent businessperson, and I truly liked people. But I couldn't seem to get the hang of the whole socializing bit. I wondered if something was "wrong" with me.

I began the process of self-discovery and research several years ago, and I'm convinced more than ever that shyness is a symptom and introversion is the source. Introversion is not a disease—quite the contrary—but it can certainly be viewed as a handicap in an extroverted world.

In order to be effective in my job (I'm in a very extroverted job that involves talking to people most of the day), I've learned a number of things that have helped me to accept and "manage" my introversion.

Nothing is wrong with me. I have lots to offer to others because I'm an introvert, and I cannot, and should not, change who I am. But I can become more effective in my interactions with others.

I have learned to be extroverted if needed. If I anticipate a period of extroversion that involves a difficult discussion or confrontation, I will often rehearse it mentally or in writing. However, I must schedule a counterbalance (quiet and solace) following times of extroversion in order to recharge my batteries.

I must assess the "audience" with which I am interacting and adapt my behavior accordingly when dealing with an extrovert. I should not expect the extrovert to adapt to me. I adapt to them to communicate better.

I will place myself in situations that require me to strengthen my weak extroversion "muscle." For example, I volunteer for leadership positions for which I am uncomfortable in order to develop more expertise in dealing with others. I force myself to speak up in meetings rather than sitting by passively.

I look for tips and techniques to help me feel at ease making the small talk that extroverts enjoy. When the necessity arises, I can become a "pseudoextrovert." Much to my pleasure, once I get the conversation started, the extrovert will typically do the majority of talking. Because I genuinely like people, I listen and appreciate that I've gotten to know someone better or made a new friend. I would have missed out on that opportunity if I did not make the first approach.

I encourage my children's extroversion even though it is uncomfortable at times. However, I also try to teach them to be sensitive to the introverts in their lives, like their mother, and to recognize that a person's need for times of solitude is just another way of approaching life.

Thank you for your work in this area. I've gained so much from reading your materials and look forward with anticipation to your new book on shyness.

–Cheryl Mostrom

Appendix B
100 Self-Knowledge Questions

The following questions will help you learn to know yourself better.

1. What is an ideal relationship to me?
2. What do I think about most when I'm just standing in a queue?
3. What are my qualities I'm most proud of? Least proud of?
4. If I won the lottery, what would I do with the money?
5. What was the last argument I had? Why? What good points did the other person have?
6. What do I like about children in general and what don't I like about them?
7. Physically, what do I feel are my best features? My worst?
8. What cause or charity is the most important to me?
9. What is "honor" to me? Am I honorable?
10. Who is the God of my understanding?
11. What is my definition of "success" for me? Am I successful?
12. What influence did my parents have on me? Siblings? Other relatives?
13. If I had only a few months to live, how would I spend them?
14. What does art mean to the world? To me?
15. Do I think most people lie a little? A lot?
16. Who is my best friend? Why?
17. Am I a morning, afternoon, or night person? How do I feel in each part of the day?
18. If I could live in any era, which would it be? Why?
19. What does loyalty mean to me? Am I a loyal person?
20. How do I believe the universe was created?
21. What do I think is our country's influence around the world? Is that influence good?

22. What do I see my life being like when I am very old?

23. How do I feel about industrial air pollution versus progress?

24. What do I most like about my job? Least like?

25. If I could afford to collect anything, what would I collect?

26. What do I think happens after death?

27. What is my favorite film? Television show? Why?

28. If I could live in any city in the world except mine, which would it be?

29. How do I feel about what's happening in the environment now?

30. What do I think is the cause of most relationships failing?

31. Are things in life "predestined"? Do we have completely free will?

32. What really gets me angry? Why?

33. What do I think the future of the computer is? The Web?

34. What makes a leader? Am I a leader?

35. What are my favorite books? Who are my favorite authors? Why?

36. Do I prefer living in the city or the country? Why?

37. What public figure, past or present, do I admire most?

38. Whom do I admire most in my personal life?

39. How do I define "spirituality"? Am I a spiritual person?

40. What are my Top-10 favorite websites? Why?

41. How do I feel about animal testing if it is used to create a product to help humans?

42. Did I have a happy childhood?

43. What do I think the human brain is capable of?

44. If I won a ticket to travel anywhere in the world, where would I go? Why?

45. If I could be famous, what would I want to be famous for?

46. What's really important to me? Family? Job? Community? Other?

47. What are my favorite foods? Least favorite? Am I a good cook?

48. What is my favorite song? Singer? Band? Why?

49. What's the best thing about being the age I am? The worst?

50. How are kids growing up with the Internet going to be different from previous generations?
51. What is my opinion of my hometown's most popular newspaper?
52. What three things would I like to change about me?
53. What is my worst fear?
54. Should couples live together before marriage? Why?
55. Can I tell if somebody is lying? How?
56. Do I procrastinate too much? If so, on what and why?
57. How do I feel about meditation?
58. Do children need both a mother and a father to grow up healthy?
59. If I could change just one thing in my life, what would it be?
60. What are my dreams like? Do they mean anything?
61. What relevance do the ancient philosophers have for today's way of life?
62. How do I feel about school reunions?
63. Do I have any limiting patterns? If so, what could I do to change them?
64. What role does music play in my life?
65. How do I feel about television violence? Sex?
66. Am I a "dog person" or a "cat person," or do I prefer any other animal as pets?
67. How do I feel about the "institution of marriage" in general?
68. How do I feel about marriage for me? Will it/has it been good?
69. Am I superstitious? If so, about what–and why?
70. What was my first job, and what did it mean to me?
71. Do I have any phobias? Claustrophobia? Vertigo? Others?
72. Do I think we should limit world population in some way?
73. Do I believe in unconditional love?
74. If I had to live in confinement with just one thing, what would it be? Why?
75. Do I think people are basically good or bad? Why?
76. Should infomercials be banned? Why?

77. What is my favorite sport to play? To watch? What do I like about it?

78. How much do I believe of what I hear on TV newscasts? Read in newspapers?

79. Should we have legislation limiting buying foreign products versus domestic?

80. Are political elections fair? Why?

81. Do I believe any of the popular diets work?

82. Which world leader do I feel has had the most positive effect on humanity?

83. If I could speak another language, what would it be? Why?

84. How do I feel about eating meat versus vegetarianism?

85. How do I feel about assisted suicide?

86. Should people know their family tree? Why?

87. What is my favorite television show? Why?

88. What is my favorite subject to talk about?

89. Were/are my parents happy?

90. Do I believe in reincarnation? Why?

91. What is my stand on abortion and right to life?

92. How do I feel about "finding love online"?

93. How do I feel about our educational system? Why?

94. How do I truly feel about each of my family members at this time?

95. Am I happy? Why?

96. Do I have a satisfying sex life? Why?

97. At what age should someone retire? How about me?

98. Do I prefer traveling by train, plane, bus, or car? Why?

99. Who do/did I love most (father, mother, siblings, lover, best friend, other)? Why?

100. How do I feel about my life right now?

Now write more questions, then more, so you can answer one every day of your life.

Acknowledgments

A BIG thank-you to the following Shys who took the time to share their very poignant stories with me. I pray that *Good-Bye to Shy* helps and that your stories all have happy endings.

Alexandra T., Manning, South Carolina
Alexia P., Chicago, Illinois
Aliia P., Darwin, Australia
Alisa L., Washington, D.C.
Alison M., Sydney, Australia
Allison D., Canberra, Australia
Alvin V., Sarasota, Florida
Amanda R., Columbus, Ohio
Amber T., New Castle, England
Amy P., Sidney, Australia
Andrew D., London, England
Andy H., Clearwood, Florida
Angela P., Hope, Arkansas
Anna E., Tenby, Wales
Antony T., Liverpool, England
Ariana G., Taos, New Mexico
Babs J., Chandler, Arizona
Barb G., Phoenix, Arizona
Ben K., Clarksville, Tennessee
Beth P., Carlow, Ireland
Bob I., Phoenix, Arizona
Boris Z., Moscow, Russia
Brigette S., Englewood, Florida
Brittany V., Logan, West Virginia
Bruce P., Boulder, Colorado

Buddy K., Los Angeles, California

Burt F., Wilmington, Delaware

Candace L., Houston, Texas

Candy G., Jacksonville, Florida

Carrie B., Jacksonville, Florida

Chelsea W., Canberra, Australia

Cheryl M., Phoenix, Arizona

Chris O., Hartford, Connecticut

Chris T., Great Bend, Indiana

Chris U., Silver Spring, Maryland

Claire F., Bloomfield, Vermont

Coral B., Hudson, Florida

Courtney U., Limerick, Ireland

Curt H., Eugene, Oregon

Dalton H., Wellington, New Zealand

Dan Y., London, England

Dana J., Wellington, New Zealand

Daniel T., London, England

Danielle L., Greenwich, Connecticut

Darla P., Beaver, Pennsylvania

Darlene N., Los Angeles, California

Dave B., Toledo, Ohio

Dave F., Providence, Rhode Island

David D., Great Falls, Montana

Dean P., London, England

Deeana P., Claremont, New Hampshire

Denise D., Sitka, Alaska

Diana L., Melbourne, Australia

Diana P., Lindenhurst, New York

Diane F., Delta, Alabama

Diane M., Chicago, Illinois

Dimitri D., Athens, Greece

Dina B., Topeka, Kansas

Don G., Lindenhurst, New York

Don M., Baker, California

Donna I., Port Huron, Michigan

Donna J., Martinsburg, West Virginia

Doug S., Inverness, Scotland

Drew P., Wellington, New Zealand

Dusty P., Brighton, England

Eric P., Beverly Hills, California

Fanny T., Baltimore, Maryland

Felicia G., Dallas, Texas

Felicia H., San Francisco, California

Fred H., Baltimore, Maryland

Fred P., Baltimore, Maryland

Gail F., Poughkeepsie, New York

Gail H., Kansas City, Missouri

Gatsah W., Capetown, South Africa

Geoffrey F., Auckland, New Zealand

Greg L., Agoura, California

Greg P., Lyons, Nebraska

Haley U., Edinburgh, Scotland

Hannah R., Conwy, Wales

Holly K., Brisbane, Australia

Holly P., Wellington, New Zealand

Ian H., Baltimore, Maryland

Jacques C., Athens, Greece

James S., Vancouver, Canada

Jean S., Miami, Florida

Jeannie D., Tampa, Florida

Jennie H., Idaho Falls, Idaho

Jeremy B., Abilene, Texas

Ken K., Beaver Falls, Pennsylvania

Koos V., Pretoria, South Africa

Linda G., Carrollton, Ohio

Michael D., London, England

Pennant L., London, England

Ralph G., Greenville, Kentucky

Sandra V., Lexington, Mississippi

Sarah F., Northampton, Massachusetts

Stephen S., Los Angeles, California

Tony V., Sydney, Australia

Will H., Chicago, Illinois

A special thanks to my fabulous editor, Judith McCarthy at McGraw-Hill (Judith, you're the best!). And to my very special copyeditor, Lisa Stracks, who helped me organize my thoughts as well as my abysmal punctuation.

References

1. Philip G. Zimbardo, *Shyness, What It Is, What to Do About It* (Reading, MA: Perseus Books, 1977).
2. *Enable* (the magazine of The American Association of People with Disabilities).
3. R. C. Kessler et al., "Lifetime and 12-Month Prevalence of DSM-III-R Psychiatric Disorders in the United States," *Archives of General Psychiatry* 51 (1994): 8–19.
4. Philip Zimbardo, "The Social Disease Called Shyness," *Psychology Today* (August 1975).
5. F. Schneider et al., "Subcortical Correlates of Differential Classical Conditioning of Adversive Emotional Reactions in Social Phobia," *Journal of Behavioral Research Therapy* 45 (1999): 863–71.
6. Schneider et al., "Subcortical Correlates," 863–71.
7. Zimbardo, *Shyness*.
8. L. Fehm and J. Margraf, "Thought Suppression: Specificity in Agoraphobia Versus Broad Impairment in Social Phobia?" *Journal of Behavioral Research Therapy* 40 (2002): 57–66.
9. R. P. Mattick, A. C. Page, and L. Lampe, "Cognitive and Behavioral Aspects," in *Social Phobia: Clinical and Research Perspectives*, ed. M. B. Stein, 189–229 (Washington, DC: American Psychiatric Press, 1995).
10. Fehm and Margraf, "Thought Suppression," 57–66.
11. Claudia M. Roebers, U. Wuerzburg, and Wolfgang Schneider, "Individual Differences in Children's Eyewitness Recall: The Influence of Intelligence and Shyness," *Applied Developmental Science* 5, no. 1 (2001): 9–20.
12. S. Rachman, J. Gruter-Andrew, and R. Shafran, "Post-Event Processing in Social Anxiety," *Journal of Behavioral Research Therapy* 38 (2000): 611–17.
13. W. M. Bukowsky, B. Hoza, and M. Boivin, "Popularity, Friendship, and Emotional Adjustment During Early Adolescence," *New Directions in Child Development* 60 (Summer 1993): 23–37.

14. L. Stopa and D. M. Clark, "Social Phobia and the Interpretation of Social Events," *Journal of Behavioral Research Therapy* 38 (2000): 273–83.

15. A. T. Beck and D. A. Clark, "An Information Processing Model of Anxiety: Automatic and Strategic Processes," *Journal of Behavioral Research Therapy* 35 (1997): 49–58.

16. Robin Foster Cappe and Lynne E. Alden, "A Comparison of Treatment Strategies for Clients Functionally Impaired by Extreme Shyness and Social Avoidance," *Journal of Consulting and Clinical Psychology* 54, no. 6: 796–801.

17. Schneider et al., "Subcortical Correlates," 863–71.

18. John R. Marshall, M.D., *Social Phobia* (New York: Basic Books, 1994).

19. Mark Pollack, M.D., Naomi M. Simon, M.D., and Michael Otto, Ph.D., *Social Anxiety Disorder: Research and Practice* (New York: Professional Publishing Group, 2003).

20. Pollack, Simon, and Otto, *Social Anxiety Disorder*.

21. Zimbardo, *Shyness*.

22. Zimbardo, *Shyness*.

23. L. Festinger, *A Theory of Cognitive Dissonance* (Stanford, CA: Stanford University Press, 1957).

24. Margaret Bald, "Organizing the Shy: VVM, the Association of Shy People in the Netherlands," *World Press Review* (1 November 1998): 38.

25. Jonathan Berent, *Beyond Shyness* (New York: Simon & Schuster, 1993).

26. Zimbardo, *Shyness*.

27. Zimbardo, *Shyness*.

28. M. A. Bruch, M. Fallon, and R. G. Heimberg, "Social Phobia and Difficulties in Occupational Adjustment," *Journal of Counseling Psychology* 50 (2003): 109–17.

29. A. Wells, D. M. Clark, P. Salovskis et al., "Social Phobia: The Role of In-situation Safety Behaviors in Maintaining Anxiety and Negative Beliefs," *Journal of Behavioral Therapy* 26 (1995): 153–61.

30. M. R. Otto et al., "Alcohol Dependence in Panic Disorder Patients," *Journal of Psychiatric Research* 26 (1992): 29–38.

31. F. R. Schneier et al., "Alcohol Abuse and Social Phobia," *Journal of Anxiety Disorders* 3 (1989): 15–23.

32. H. Arkowitz et al., "The Behavioural Assessment of Social Competence in Males," *Behavioral Therapy* 6 (1975): 3–13.

33. Signe A. Dayhoff, Ph.D., *Diagonally Parked in a Parallel Universe* (Placitas, New Mexico: Effectiveness-Plus Publications, 2000).

34. Bernardo J. Carducci, Ph.D., *Shyness: A Bold New Approach* (New York: HarperCollins, 1999).

35. Judith Martin, *Miss Manners' Guide for the Turn-of-the-Millennium* (New York: Fireside, 1990).

36. Zimbardo, *Shyness.*

37. Zimbardo, *Shyness.*

38. Zimbardo, *Shyness.*

39. Elaine N. Aron, Ph.D., *The Highly Sensitive Person in Love* (New York: Broadway Books, 2000).

40. Aron, *The Highly Sensitive Person in Love.*

41. P. J. Cooper and M. Eke, "Childhood Shyness and Maternal Social Phobia: A Community Study," *British Journal of Psychiatry* 174 (1999): 439–43.

42. As cited in Berent, *Beyond Shyness.*

43. W. H. Jones, J. M. Cheek, and S. R. Briggs (Eds.), *Shyness: Perspectives on Research and Treatment* (New York: Springer, 1986).

44. Aron, *The Highly Sensitive Person in Love.*

45. W. J. Goode, "The Theoretical Importance of Love," *American Sociological Review* 2 (1959): 38–47.

46. Timothy Perper, *Sex Signals: The Biology of Love* (Philadelphia: ISI Press, 1985).

47. M. M. Moore, "Nonverbal Courtship Patterns in Women: Context and Consequences," *Ethnology and Sociobiology* 6 (1985): 237–47.

48. Joan Kellerman et al., "Looking and Loving: The Effects of Mutual Gaze on Feelings of Romantic Love," *Journal of Research in Personality* 23 (1989): 145–61.

49. Helen Fisher, *Anatomy of Love* (New York: Fawcett Columbine, 1992).

50. Zick Rubin, "Measurement of Romantic Love," *Journal of Personality and Social Psychology* 16 (1970): 265–73.

51. Donn Byrne, *The Attraction Paradigm* (New York: Academic Press, 1971).

52. Mark Cook and Robert McHenry, *Sexual Attraction* (New York: Pergamon Press, 1978).

53. John M. Townsend and Gary D. Levy, "Effects of Potential Partner's Physical Attractiveness and Socioeconomic Status on Sexuality and Partner Selection," *Archives of Sexual Behavior* 19, no. 2 (1992): 149–64.

54. Townsend and Levy, "Effects of Physical Attractiveness," 149–64.

55. Bernardo Carducci and Philip Zimbardo, "Are You Shy?" *Psychology Today* (November/December 1995).

56. Zimbardo, *Shyness*.

57. J. Kagan, J. S. Reznick, and N. Snidman, "Biological Bases of Childhood Shyness," *Science* 240 (1988): 167–71.

58. Steve Campbell, *Third and Long: Men's Playbook for Solving Marital/Relationship Problems and Building a Winning Team* (Bloomington, IN: Authorhouse, 2005).

59. L. K. Silverman, "Parenting Young Gifted Children," in *Intellectual Giftedness in Young Children*, ed. J. R. Whitmore (New York: The Haworth Press, 1986).

60. Carducci and Zimbardo, "Are You Shy?"

61. Cooper and Eke, "Childhood Shyness and Maternal Social Phobia," 439–43.

62. L. Ost, "Ways of Acquiring Phobias and Outcome of Behavioral Treatments," *Journal of Behavioral Research Therapy* 23 (1985): 683–89.

63. R. Stemberger, S. Turner, D. Beidel et al., "Social Phobia: An Analysis of Possible Developmental Factors," *Journal of Abnormal Psychology* 104 (1995): 526–31.

64. A. R. Taylor, "Predictors of Peer Rejection in Early Elementary Grades: Roles of Problem Behavior, Academic Achievement, and Teacher Preference," *Journal of Clinical Child Psychology* 18 (1989): 360–65.

65. Taylor, "Predictors of Peer Rejection," 360–65.

66. B. F. Chorpita and D. H. Barlow, "The Development of Anxiety: The Role of Control in the Early Environment," *Psychology Bulletin* 124 (1998): 3–21.

67. J. Belsky, K.-H. Hsieh, and K. Crnic, "Mothering, Fathering, and Infant Negativity as Antecedents of Boys' Externalizing Problems and Inhibition at Age 3 Years: Differential Susceptibility to Rearing Experience?" *Journal of Developmental Psychopathology* 10 (1998): 301–19.

68. P. A. Pilkonis, C. Heape, and R. H. Klein, "Treating Shyness and Other Psychiatric Difficulties in Psychiatric Outpatients," *Communication Education* 29 (1980): 250–55.

Recommended Reading

Anthony, M. M. (1976). *Ten Simple Solutions to Shyness: How to Overcome Shyness, Social Anxiety, and Fear of Public Speaking.* Oakland, CA: New Harbinger Publications.

Bower, S. A. and Bower, G. H. (1976). *Asserting Yourself.* Menlo Park, CA: Addison-Wesley.

Cheek, J. M. (1990). *Conquering Shyness.* New York: Basic Books.

Carducci, B. J. (1999). *Shyness: A Bold New Approach.* New York: Harper-Collins.

Gabor, D. (1983). *How to Start a Conversation and Make Friends.* New York: Fireside Books.

Leary, M. R. & Kowalski, R. M. (1995). *Social Anxiety.* New York: Guilford Press.

Markway, G. B., Carmin, C. N., Pollard, C. A., and Flynn, T. (1992). *Dying of Embarrassment: Help for Social Anxiety and Phobia.* Oakland, CA: New Harbinger.

McKay, M. and Fanning, P. (1987). *Self-Esteem.* Oakland, CA: New Harbinger Publications.

Schneier, F. and Welkowitz, L. (1996). *The Hidden Face of Shyness: Understanding and Overcoming Social Anxiety.* New York: Avon Books.

Smith, M. J. (1975). *When I Say No I Feel Guilty.* New York: Bantam Books.

Zimbardo, P. G. (1977; Reprinted, 1996). *Shyness: What It Is, What to Do About It.* Reading, MA: Addison-Wesley.

Zimbardo, P. G. and Radl, S. L. (1981). *The Shy Child.* New York: McGraw-Hill.

Index

About the Author

Leil Lowndes, a recovered Shy, is an internationally acclaimed communications expert and author of the bestselling *How to Talk to Anyone*. She coaches top executives of Fortune 500 companies and government agencies to become more effective communicators

She has spoken in every major city in the United States and regularly conducts shyness workshops. In addition to engrossing audiences on hundreds of TV and radio shows, her work has been acclaimed by the *New York Times*, the *Chicago Tribune*, and *Time* magazine. She is the author of eight books including the top-selling *How to Make Anyone Fall in Love with You* and the award-winning audio program *Conversation Confidence*. Her articles have appeared in professional journals and popular publications such as *Vogue*, *Men's Health*, *Reader's Digest*, *Penthouse*, *Redbook*, and *Psychology Today*.

To sign up for Leil's complimentary monthly communications hint, go to her Web page: www.lowndes.com.

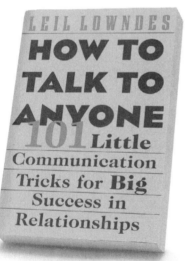